—LOST LINES—
BIRMINGHAM
and the
BLACK COUNTRY
NIGEL WELBOURN

Ian Allan
PUBLISHING

Contents

First published 2002
Reprinted 2006

ISBN 0 7110 2844 3

Published by Ian Allan Publishing

an imprint of Ian Allan Publishing Ltd, Hersham, Surrey KT12 4RG.
Printed by Ian Allan Printing Ltd, Hersham, Surrey KT12 4RG.

Code: 0604/3

Cover photographs courtesy of Colour-Rail

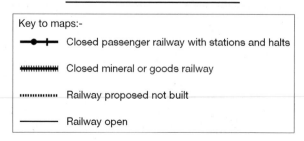

Key to maps:-

━●┼━ Closed passenger railway with stations and halts

╫╫╫╫╫╫ Closed mineral or goods railway

·············· Railway proposed not built

──── Railway open

Introduction

I first arrived in Birmingham in 1966. New Street station was in the course of demolition and the adjoining Queens Hotel was a mere derelict shell. At that time it looked as if the remaining railways in Birmingham and the Black Country had a bleak future. They were inextricably linked to the heavy industries in the area and many of these were in a state of terminal decline. It was an area where most people used the car or the bus to travel to work. The railways were duplicated on several routes and had suffered from years of lack of investment that had led to many dirty and often desolate stations being served infrequently by equally dingy and aged trains. The whole area was ripe for the infamous Beeching axe to fall.

Closures went ahead, while on some surviving lines a skeleton passenger service made closure seem inevitable. I later recall travelling from Snow Hill to Wolverhampton Low Level on the single remaining track of the former GWR main line, in a single-coach 'Bubblecar'. There were few passengers and at one point the driver was forced to leave the train to remove an old pram deliberately placed on the line. It seemed unlikely that this once great network of lines would ever play a major role in the area again. The motorway age had arrived; the majority of railways, as with the canals before them, would be consigned to the history books, or would they?

The rebuilt New Street station heralded a new beginning. A network once congested with freight trains has become increasingly congested with passenger trains. The nature and pattern of employment in the area is changing, commerce is replacing manufacturing and there is today

Below: Entering the Black Country en route to Birmingham. Steam still lingered on relief and seasonal workings when this view was taken on 7 May 1963. In this scene the Wolverhampton Low Level stationmaster chats to the driver of 'Castle' class No 7001 *Sir James Milne*, as the Stafford Road engine awaits the rightaway with a southbound 'Pines Express'. *Ian Allan Library*

considerable growth of commuting, particularly to Birmingham city centre.

Forty years on and the gloom of the 1960s has gone; expansion and improvement are to be seen everywhere. I recently travelled on a packed Midland Metro tramcar using much of the ex-GWR route to Wolverhampton; the transformation would have been unbelievable in the 1960s. Birmingham and the Black Country have seen many changes, including the end of much of the area's blackness. The loss of some railways and a rationalisation of most remaining lines have been part of this process.

This book covers those lines that are lost in the area, but in keeping with other books in the Lost Lines series, some former railway lines and facilities have been included for their wider historical or geographical associations with the area.

Abbreviations	
BR	British Railways
GJR	Grand Junction Railway
GWR	Great Western Railway
L&B	London & Birmingham Railway
LMR	London Midland Region of British Railways
LMS	London, Midland & Scottish Railway
LNWR	London & North Western Railway
MR	Midland Railway
OWWR	Oxford, Worcester & Wolverhampton Railway
SSR	South Staffordshire Railway
WR	Western Region of British Railways

Above: The area made everything from 'a pin to a steam engine'. Here, the GWR works at Wolverhampton Stafford Road shows the engine erecting shop in August 1932 after its expansion had been completed. Although locomotives were no longer built here at this time, heavy repairs were undertaken. The distinctive and famous GWR brass safety valve cowl, fitted to all GWR locomotives, was designed at Wolverhampton. The works closed in June 1964. *Ian Allan Library*

Right: The railways came to an understanding with the canals. In Birmingham, the Worcester & Birmingham Canal had to be diverted, to allow a line to reach the Midland Railway's central Birmingham goods depot at Suffolk Street. The Holiday Street aqueduct was built by the Midland Railway and completed in 1885 to carry the diverted canal. This view was taken from underneath the structure in August 2001. *Author*

1 A Black History

It is difficult to imagine that at one time the great metropolis of Birmingham, together with the urban and industrial expanses of the Black Country, was simply rolling green English countryside and woodland. Although metal working and mining stretch back some 500 years, the area was transformed by the Industrial Revolution from tranquil farmland to an area described in 1868 as 'black by day and red by night'. The sheer number of iron furnaces in the area created a red glow at night and filled the air with smoke and soot. This, together with the waste heaps created, helped to give the buildings and the area its Black Country label.

Natural resources of ironstone and limestone, together with 'thick coal', were the main ingredients of development. Originally plentiful seams of coal, sometimes up to 40ft thick, could be found just below ground. The area developed into a great workshop of a thousand trades, with everything from a pin to a steam engine being produced. The area gave birth to an equal number of inventions, and Thomas Newcomen built the world's first successful stationary steam engine as far back as 1712.

Not itself part of the Black Country, it is perhaps surprising that Birmingham, which lacked significant natural resources and natural transport routes, became the most notable powerhouse of the Industrial Revolution. The whole relatively small area of Birmingham and the Black Country developed rapidly during Victorian times and Birmingham became the second largest city in Britain.

The area's growth was initially made possible by the development of canals. The first canal to serve Birmingham, in 1769, was from Wednesbury and the last to reach the city was completed in 1844. The canals allowed both raw materials and finished goods to travel in and out of the area more cheaply than previously, giving great impetus to the industrialisation of the area.

A network of about 250 miles of narrow lock canals developed and the area became known as the Venice of England. Although far inland, canals and rivers provided links to the main seaports, and the world's first iron steamship was built at Tipton. The hydraulic jacks to launch Brunel's ship the *Great Eastern* were designed at Smethwick and the huge anchors and chains for the *Titanic* were made at Netherton.

Although prone to water shortages in summer and to freezing over in winter, the canals remained in use for freight after the railways opened and several connections between canal basins and the railways were developed. However, the canals could not compete with the railways and many offered themselves up to the railway companies; thus it was that the Birmingham Canal Navigations became part of the LNWR in 1846. Gradually the canals declined. In the 1950s most rail interchange traffic ended, while by the 1960s most freight use had also ceased. It is estimated that about a quarter are now completely abandoned, but the decline has been halted and there is an ever-growing leisure use of those canals that remain in Birmingham and the Black Country.

The mineral reserves and growing industrial wealth of the area attracted railways, and a number of early mineral lines were developed to connect collieries to factories, or to canals. In 1829, the Shutt End Railway was built to carry coal from Shutt End to the Ashwood Basin on the Staffordshire & Worcestershire Canal. The line utilised steam traction over part of the route and the locomotive *Agenoria* was built in Stourbridge, while at the same time a sister engine, *The Stourbridge Lion*, was the first steam locomotive to be exported to America. Remarkably, both engines have been preserved.

There was opposition to the new railways from the canals, stagecoaches, turnpike roads and landowners. Indeed some towns felt they were doing just fine without railways and were far from enthusiastic about the new form of transport. Nevertheless, the first passenger railway and trunk line arrived in the form of the Grand Junction Railway. Its route from Liverpool skirted Wolverhampton and Walsall, to reach Birmingham in July 1837. This was followed shortly

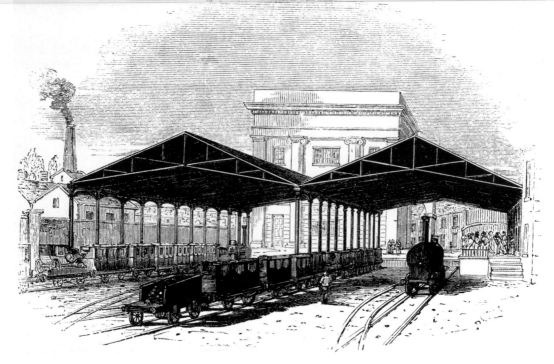

after by the triumphant arrival of the London & Birmingham Railway in September 1838.

The London & Birmingham Railway was built to the grand scale and the line ran into its well-built Curzon Street station at Birmingham. This included a building of classical design that towered above the brick houses in the area. Unlike the original fine buildings at Euston, it survives to this day. The Grand Junction and London & Birmingham lines soon linked up at Birmingham. A link to Gloucester was provided by August 1841 and a direct line to Derby, promoted by Birmingham businessmen, opened in February 1842 and began to give Birmingham junction status in the early national railway network.

The Grand Junction and the London & Birmingham railways initially found themselves at loggerheads over a number of issues, but the threat of the Great Western's broad, 7ft gauge encroachment into the area led to their merger and the creation of the London & North Western Railway.

Years of railway growth were to follow and although there were no immense physical difficulties to overcome, construction was not always straightforward. Fights between rival company's navvies sometimes resulted in the use of the Riot Act. The blockading of new lines and financial uncertainty were all aspects of the colourful railway history of the area. The railways did more than anything to shape and expand the region, providing local and through routes in and around an ever-growing industrial area.

Yet even from the railway's inception, closures went ahead. The withdrawal of passenger services from Bromford Forge station took place in May 1843 and

from Portobello and Wednesfield Heath stations in January 1873.

The most extensive 3ft 6in gauge tram system in Britain developed in the area. Although the trams did not create the conditions for industrialisation and growth to the same extent as the canals and railways, they did shape the suburban development of many settlements. The first trams in the area were horse-drawn and dated from the 1870s. Steam was used in the 1880s, but electric trams were being used on almost all routes by 1904, and the last steam tram ran in 1906. Trams were also able to serve all parts of the area and cable-operated tramcars were used on hilly sections between Birmingham and Handsworth to cope with the steep gradients.

Municipally operated lines came to provide the majority of services in the area and provided stiff competition for the railways as frequent electric services, together with one-penny fares for workmen, ate into railway revenues. In turn, the flexibility and economics of bus operation began to reduce the tram's profitability. Although in the 1930s Birmingham still had almost 800 tramcars, Wolverhampton had lost its trams in 1928.

The first electric trolleybuses were introduced in Birmingham in 1922 and in Wolverhampton the following year. 'Trolleys' used the overhead equipment of many former tram routes in Birmingham and the Black Country. This silent and non-polluting form of electric transport saw the remaining tram systems close in the area completely by 1953, but by 1967 the last trolleybus had also run. The trams returned in 1999 with the opening of the first route of the Midland Metro between Wolverhampton and Birmingham.

Left: The L&B Curzon Street terminus station at Birmingham was designed by Philip Hardwick and opened in 1838. This view of the iron train sheds, which covered six tracks, was taken from Osborne's *London to Birmingham Railway Guide*. The station was one of the earliest of any size to close to regular passenger traffic, as far back as July 1854. *Ian Allan Library*

Upper right: The original stations at Birmingham were found to be too small, almost as soon as they opened, but the station constructed at New Street and opened in 1854, befitted the second city of the Empire. It was built on an altogether larger scale as seen in this view, taken c1900, of the four centre roads, Post Office subways and footbridges on the LNWR side of the station, looking towards Wolverhampton. *Ian Allan Library*

Centre right: Birmingham Corporation tram No 405, on route 41, is seen here in the centre of Birmingham. This tramcar was built in 1912 and withdrawn by 1949. In 1953, all the remaining routes, on a once extensive, 80-mile network of 3ft 6in gauge tramways, were closed. *Ian Allan Library*

Lower right: The Oxford, Worcester & Wolverhampton Railway started some work on Dudley Tunnel in 1846. About seven million bricks were used in its construction and it was completed in 1849, but financial problems meant that the line was not open to regular passenger traffic until 1852. When this view was taken, the tunnel was in use and the cutting vegetation well maintained. Today, the tunnel is out of use and the signal and platelayers' hut have gone, but tracks remain for a possible reopening of the line for freight. *Ian Allan Library*

2 Rationalisation and Retrenchment

The wealth of the region attracted railways, while the location of the area in the centre of England meant that it became a railway crossroads. The numerous smaller companies were gradually amalgamated and three main railway companies developed to serve the region.

The formation of the LNWR in 1846 from the London & Birmingham and Grand Junction railways laid the foundations for one of the more powerful pre-Grouping railways. The South Staffordshire Railway penetrated the north of the Black Country, but in 1867 it also became part of the LNWR. Passenger and freight growth was considerable and the Birmingham station at Curzon Street soon proved too small and was replaced by New Street in June 1854. The LNWR provided a bypass route to the area, via the Trent Valley, which helped relieve pressure, but Birmingham remained important, and the Stour Valley line linking Birmingham and Wolverhampton was particularly busy. LNWR lines have survived relatively well in the area, although the Harborne branch closed, together with the ex-LNWR lines in the Dudley area.

Left: The 4.20pm freight train from Wichnor, seen here shunting at Norton Junction on 20 May 1950, with ex-LNWR 0-8-0 No 49371 in charge. The pole held by the employee standing beside the engine was used to join or separate the loose-coupled wagons. *P. B. Whitehouse*

Left: Ex-MR Class 3 0-6-0 No 43263, with a Worcester-bound parcels train passing the site of the then closed Five Ways station in May 1953, on the ex-Birmingham West Suburban Railway. The station subsequently reopened in 1978. The bridge on the right of this view was over the freight-only line to the Midland Railway's central Birmingham goods depot at Suffolk Street. *P. B. Whitehouse*

The Midland Railway was formed in 1844. By absorbing the Birmingham & Gloucester Railway, the Midland effectively thwarted the GWR broad gauge from obtaining a major foothold in the Birmingham area. The MR's Birmingham Lawley Street station closed to passengers in May 1851, when services were transferred to Curzon Street, which in turn closed three years later when New Street station opened. Congestion on the network grew and by 1885 an extension was added to New Street station, to give the MR its own platforms. Early passenger closures on ex-MR routes were implemented by the LMS following the Grouping in 1923. They closed the link to Brownhills in 1930, the Walsall-Wolverhampton services the following year, and the Birmingham circular suburban services, via Lifford and Moseley, in 1941.

The GWR opened its line to Birmingham from Banbury in October 1852, while the Oxford, Worcester & Wolverhampton Railway reached Wolverhampton in July 1854. The OWWR was eventually absorbed by the GWR, which aimed to expand its broad gauge line in the area and to complete its main line to London. However, the broad gauge was prevented from expanding by the Gauge Act and the GWR was frustrated in its attempts to

build a joint station with the LNWR at Birmingham. Nevertheless, the GWR provided its own station at Birmingham and at other main centres and developed an extensive network of standard gauge lines in the area. The greatest ex-GWR losses were under BR in the 1960s. The former main lines from Birmingham and Stourbridge to Wolverhampton were major casualties, together with the substantial ex-GWR stations in Wolverhampton and Birmingham.

Below: A Sunday engineering working at Birmingham Snow Hill station, hauled by ex-GWR 'Dukedog' 4-4-0 No 9001. The engine was built in 1936, incorporating parts from earlier 4-4-0s. The train is seen here leaving the north end of Platform 6, heading a train of empty ballast wagons, forming a through working to Oswestry, on 13 September 1953. A tank locomotive waits at the adjacent platform, one of two bays at the north end of the station between the main and relief line platforms. *E. D. Bruton*

When the railways were merged in 1923 into the 'Big Four', the GWR was the only one to retain its original identity. The LNWR and the MR both became part of the LMS. The LMS was to dominate much of the area, and its extensive freight operations, particularly from coal, were to provide the main profits for its shareholders. World War 2 had a major effect on all the railways in the area. They were worked hard with minimum investment and air raids caused considerable damage. Both the LMS and GWR emerged from the war in a run-down condition.

Thus it was in 1948 that all the railways were merged into the single nationalised British Railways. The lines in the area were at first divided between two regions of BR, the Western Region and the London Midland Region, on similar boundaries to the old LMS and GWR but in 1963 the former GWR lines were transferred to the LMR. This was to cause some offence to the pride of former GWR employees, but the real rivals now came in the form of the bus, lorry and car, which were able to take advantage of the huge investment in roads and motorways then being made. As a result, many rail services were run down and became infrequent.

Left: A train arrives at Windmill End in August 1957, with an Old Hill-Dudley service. The engine at the rear of the auto trailer is '6400' class 0-6-0PT No 6422. The station was reduced to a halt in 1952, but improvements were made to the dilapidated, unlit platforms before closure in 1964. Housing development now occupies the site. *Ian Allan Library*

Right: The derelict Rubery station and the burnt out former Midland-style signalbox, looking west towards Halesowen, in February 1966. Rubery provided a passing loop on the single line between Halesowen and Longbridge. The last public passenger trains used the station in 1919, although workmen's trains to Longbridge survived until 1958, and freight until 1964. *A. Muckley*

Left: Bilston Central in March 1966, looking towards Wolverhampton, with a DMU to Birmingham Snow Hill waiting in the platform. Although there was investment in new DMUs, they were not destined to save every service and Black Country scenes such as this had great changes impending at this time. *A. Muckley*

Continued decline in the older heavier industries and in coal mining also resulted in further decreases of railway freight traffic. The changing circumstances led to a number of closures, but it was the Beeching Report in 1963 that set the foundations for the greatest losses. The report was particularly ruthless in identifying closures of passenger services to Dudley and Walsall.

Closures left Dudley without any services and originally reduced Walsall from six passenger lines to one line, while Brierley Hill, Wednesbury, West Bromwich and Cannock were to lose their passenger services altogether. Other stations survived with sparse services, Redditch having three trains a day and Bromsgrove just one.

The 1960s saw the lowest ebb for the railways in the area, but even at this time, plans for electrification and dieselisation were put forward and with the fuel crisis of 1974 further significant closures ceased. A fightback began, and a programme of reopenings and expansion was to emerge.

③ A Geographical Perspective

At a national level, in broad locational terms, Birmingham and the Black Country are to be found in the centre of a quadrilateral formed by joining the ports of London, Bristol, Liverpool and Hull. Consequently, as railways developed, the area became a junction in the heart of England and trains ran to all parts of the country.

At a regional level the area lies in the Midland Plain. The geography of the area was favourable for both canal and railway construction and several of the railways followed the earlier canal routes. At a more detailed level and perhaps uniquely, the Black Country has no clearly defined geographical boundaries, but it does broadly cover an industrial area west of Birmingham, straddling a ridge of hills running southeast from Wolverhampton. For the purposes of this book, railways with wider links to the area have been included.

The City of Birmingham never formed part of the Black Country and had none of the mineral wealth that was to be found close by. However, it cultivated strong

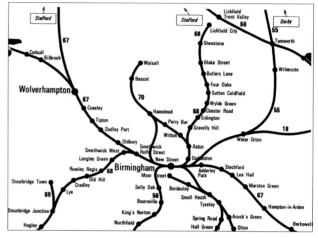

Above: A BR map of the area in 1974, after the closures of the 1960s had decimated large parts of the passenger network. *Author's collection*

Left: An LMR map of the area in 1964, with an emphasis on LMR lines to the north of Birmingham. *Author's collection*

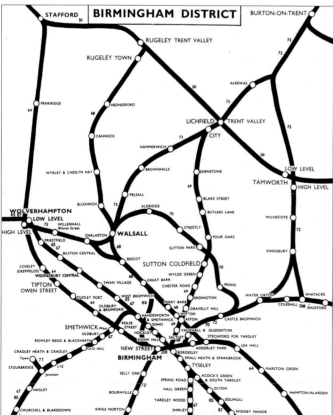

Right: One of the greatest geographical tests for motive power in the area was the climb over the Lickey Hills, with 2 miles 4 chains of 1 in 37 rising grade. In steam days, this necessitated the banking of all but the very lightest trains. Here, experimental BRCW Type 4 No D0260 *Lion* produced by a consortium, which included the Birmingham Railway Carriage & Wagon Co Ltd, pulls 16 Mk 1 coaches, some of which were also built in Birmingham, up the Lickey Incline, a load of 495 tons, on 28 May 1962. Problems with the locomotive resulted in no orders being placed and the closure of the BRCW Smethwick works. *Ian Allan Library*

links with the Black Country and developed in association with it.

Although Wolverhampton, Walsall, Dudley and Birmingham create an immense urban conglomeration, a vast network of suburban passenger lines did not develop in the area, as unlike London, the majority of the population lived and worked locally in an industrialised countryside.

Geologically the Black Country was rich in natural resources. Vast amounts of coal, black band iron ore, fire clay, sand and limestone were originally to be won. It was this mineral wealth and the absence of major physical difficulties to its extraction and transportation that led to the area becoming one of intense industrial activity. As Black Country coal deposits became depleted, coal was brought in from Cannock, but even when collieries became exhausted, dereliction, slag heaps and coal fires underground simply added to the area's reputation as the 'Black Country'.

Decline really set in after World War 1 and the area became riddled with disused industrial and mineral workings. Some parts are honeycombed with caves left from old lime workings and those at Wren's Nest, near Dudley, contain fossils known locally as Dudley Bugs! Subsidence from old mineral workings has also been a problem in some areas, and a whole lock was once lost on the Dudley Canal due to this.

In the 1930s, small pits picked a living from the dwindling coal reserves, and by 1957 only eight furnaces survived. In 1968, the last Black Country coal mine closed. At this time the area, its traditional heavy industries and its railways were in a state of decline, but ever inventive, the area turned to new developments and much of the former derelict industrial heritage and blackness has since been eliminated.

Above: A WR map of the area in 1954, relatively soon after Nationalisation, with hardly a closed route to be seen. A distinction between the WR and LMR lines in the area was apparent from this map. *Author's collection*

4 Snow Hill Sunset

The original, mainly wooden GWR station at Birmingham opened in October 1852 and was first called Snow Hill in 1858. Growth in use was almost immediate and in 1871 the station was enlarged and one of the original wooden buildings was moved to Didcot. Expansion continued and the station was completely rebuilt between 1909 and 1912, the time taken being due to operating constraints. The new station was well designed and one of the most splendid through stations in the country. It had two large island platforms with bays at the Wolverhampton end, while goods trains used two central roads. Descending grades at both ends of the platforms assisted acceleration out of the station. It was sometimes known as 'the sunshine station' because of its airy glass roof and because it was the gateway for many a holiday destination. In 1909 and 1913 power signalboxes were introduced. The station and the former hotel were damaged during air raids of 1941, but after World War 2 repairs were undertaken and the station was reglazed in 1946.

In 1953 the two-hour express train service to London was restored. The title of the one of the trains, which started at Wolverhampton, was 'The Inter-City', a title which was to inspire a railway brand name that became used throughout the world. Most local passenger services were put on regular interval timetables and were largely dieselised by 1957. A new power signalbox opened in 1960 and the station was repainted between 1958 and 1960. It was the first station in the area to use automatic tickets and the 24-hour clock.

Even had Snow Hill survived, in 1961 there were plans for a rebuild as 7½ million passengers were using the station each year at this time. As things turned out, after extensive use during the electrification of the London Midland line at New Street, the station was deliberately run down. In March 1967 the 'Blue Pullman' and other main line services came to an end. A refusal to sanction total closure meant that for a time the huge station clung to life as an unstaffed halt with

Below: 'King' class 4-6-0 No 6015 *King Richard III* with 'The Inter-City', waiting to leave Snow Hill on 20 April 1956 for Wolverhampton Low Level. The named train was first introduced between Paddington and Wolverhampton in the 1950s and later became a well-known railway brand name. The magnificent 'Kings' were taken out of service in 1962. *M. Mensing*

Right: The ornate exterior of Birmingham Snow Hill on 1 March 1967, just before closure. The buildings were originally used as a hotel, but were converted to offices in 1906, although the ground floor was retained as a restaurant. Sadly the solid white brick and stone buildings seen here were demolished in 1970. *Ian Allan Library*

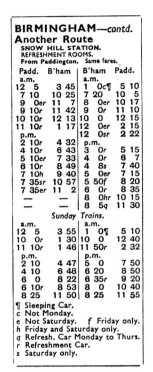

BIRMINGHAM—contd.
Another Route
SNOW HILL STATION.
REFRESHMENT ROOMS.
From Paddington.   Same fares.

Paddに	B'ham		B'ham	Padd.
a.m.			a.m.	
12 5	3 45		1 0c¶	5 10
7 10	10 25		7 20	10 5
9 0er	11 7		8 0er	10 17
9 10r	11 42		9 0r	11 10
10 10r	12 13		10 0	12 15
11 10r	1 17		12 0er	2 15
p.m.			12 0sr	2 22
2 10r	4 32		p.m.	
4 10r	6 43		3 0r	5 15
5 10er	7 33		4 0r	6 7
6 10r	8 49		4 8s	7 40
7 10h	9 40		5 0er	7 15
7 35sr	10 57		5 50f	8 20
7 35er	11 2		6 0r	8 35
—	—		8 0hr	10 15
			8 5q	11 30

Sunday Trains.

a.m.			a.m.	
12 5	3 55		1 0¶	5 10
10 0r	1 30		10 0	12 40
11 10r	1 46		11 50r	2 32
p.m.			p.m.	
2 10	4 47		5 0	7 50
4 10	6 48		6 20	8 50
6 0	8 22		6 35r	9 20
6 10r	8 53		8 0	10 40
8 25	11 50		8 25	11 55

¶ Sleeping Car.
c Not Monday.
e Not Saturday.   f Friday only.
h Friday and Saturday only.
q Refresh. Car Monday to Thurs.
r Refreshment Car.
s Saturday only.

Above: Train services April 1956. Note the sleeping cars.

Centre right: 'Manor' class 4-6-0 No 7800 *Torquay Manor* enters Snow Hill's northern approaches on 17 August 1951. The power signalbox, dating from 1909 and towering over the tracks, is just visible to the left of this busy view. Just over two decades later, not only had the entire 'Manor' class been long withdrawn from service but the same view was one of total desolation. *L. Melvill*

Right: Some LMS 'Princess Coronation' Pacifics were loaned to the WR for trials in the spring of 1955. Here, No 46237 *City of Bristol* is seen coming into a freshly white-painted Snow Hill station, with the 2.35pm Wolverhampton Low Level-Paddington train in April 1955. *B. Sackville*

two local services, but finally, in March 1972, the last train departed. After ignominious use as a car park, the neglected ruin of the once glorious station was found to be unsafe and the sun finally set on the sunshine station when demolition began in 1977.

The current modern station was built on part of the old site and was officially opened in October 1987. Not all of the old station was demolished and some remains can still be discovered around the new station. One of the clocks from Snow Hill is to be found at a Wolverhampton school. Two bench seats survive and are used on the present Snow Hill station, and a number of the distinctive BR totems are preserved. Perhaps the ghost of Dash, the GWR station dog with his collecting box, would not be too displeased with how things have turned out as in 2002, 150 years after opening, trains once again connect Snow Hill to many former GWR destinations.

Left: A few parts of the old Snow Hill station still remain. In particular the viaduct under the station that contained a maze of passages, stores and offices located beneath the platforms, as shown in this view of a small part of the former warren of facilities, taken in August 2001. *Author*

Upper right: BR Standard Class 9F 2-10-0 No 92215 trundles through Snow Hill on 28 March 1961 with a mixed freight. No 92220 of this class was the last steam locomotive built for BR in 1960. On the right is a three-car Swindon-built Cross-Country DMU. The station's white roof was beginning to look grimier in this view. *M. Mensing*

Centre right: Class 6100 2-6-2T No 6116 pauses at the signals at Snow Hill with a through freight train on 11 May 1961. These engines were built between 1931 and 1935 for London suburban services. Note the large lion and wheel, the first distinctive BR emblem, on the tank. A poster behind the locomotive advertises David Whitfield's appearance at the Birmingham Hippodrome. *D. Kingston*

G.W.R.

Birmingham
(SNOW HILL)

Left: Class 2800 2-8-0 No 2832 with a lengthy down coke freight train rumbling through Snow Hill on 2 April 1957. The freight locomotive seen here was one of a series built between 1903 and 1919. The ¼-mile length of the station and the mass of ironwork of the ridge and furrow roof are apparent from this view. *M. Mensing*

Right: BR 'Britannia' class Pacific No 70017 *Arrow* with the 5.15pm to Hereford and Cardiff, waiting to leave Snow Hill on Sunday, 9 March 1958. The engine's name perpetuated that of an earlier GWR locomotive. At this time, these engines were infrequent visitors to the station. *M. Mensing*

Left: Class 5700 0-6-0PT No 5738, one of a very large class of GWR engines. This is a Stourbridge shed locomotive and is seen here on the hazy morning of Monday, 14 September 1953, heading a stopping freight train through the middle road at Snow Hill, on the down line at the north end of the station. Note the backing signal, with two holes in its arm, on the short signal bracket, which governed the trailing crossing on the up platform road. *E. D. Bruton*

Upper right: The remaining platform for trains to Wolverhampton at Snow Hill, viewed here before complete closure in 1972. The oak-panelled refreshment room was by now boarded up. The once handsome and cheerful station had become the largest unstaffed halt in the country and was hardly an attractive, or busy, proposition when this view was taken during its last days. *Ian Allan Library*

Centre right: After closure as a through route, the gradual destruction of the station started with the removal of the former main line track and signalling, as this desolate view shows. This was an unseemly end to a fine station as the vast Snow Hill rots after closure. *Ian Allan Library*

Left: The 'Birmingham Pullman' brought a new standard of luxury to the Paddington-Wolverhampton service upon its introduction on 12 September 1960. A 'Blue Pullman' set is seen here at Snow Hill on 26 April 1965, while Stanier '8F' 2-8-0 No 48474 passes with a southbound freight. *I. Slater*

Right: A view of Snow Hill from the former central tracks. In 1970, the gap between the main platforms was filled in and used for car parking for seven years until the main demolition work began on 17 May 1977. *Ian Allan Library*

Above: Snow Hill souvenirs. The BR totem for Snow Hill was unique and a number have been saved for preservation, such as this one at the Birmingham Railway Museum at Tyseley and seen here in August 2001. *Author's collection*

Above left: The pedestrian subway that linked the main island platforms of Snow Hill with each other, looking north towards Wolverhampton, after closure of the station in 1972. The track has gone; decay and desolation can be seen everywhere. *Ian Allan Library*

Centre left: A view looking towards Snow Hill, after closure, of the main line from the 596yd Snow Hill Tunnel. Originally there was a cutting here, but it was covered over in 1874 and the Great Western Arcade was built over much of the railway formation. The tunnel could be prone to dense smoke which reduced visibility, and a clapperboard was provided to alert train drivers to the approach to the station. The derelict south power box can be seen to the left. *Ian Allan Library*

Lower left: Compare this view of Snow Hill with the activity in the earlier photographs in this chapter. The last stage of demolition, seen here on 26 May 1985, represented the sad depths to which some railways once sank in this area. *H. Frederiks*

5 Moor Street – A Suburban Survivor

The GWR built Moor Street terminus on the southern edge of Birmingham city centre to help overcome congestion at Snow Hill. It was designed primarily as a suburban station, not to be confused with the great main line Snow Hill. Moor Street opened in July 1909, but the current station, with its attractive brown terracotta tiles and modest functional style dates from 1914.

The station was on a restricted site and was thus provided with locomotive traversers for engines up to 'Castle' class size, to transfer them from one track to another. Moor Street soon became Birmingham's principal GWR suburban station and served the southern lines out of the city. The traversers were taken out of use in 1967, after the demise of steam-hauled passenger services in the area.

The closure of the southern tunnel to Snow Hill in 1968 gave Moor Street added importance for a time. Indeed, passenger use was increasing and this eventually led to the reopening of Snow Hill in 1987 and the creation of a new Moor Street station on the former through lines located to the east of the original terminus. These developments sealed the fate of the original Moor Street and it closed in September 1987.

Fortunately the passenger station buildings were listed and mothballed rather than demolished and thereby remain. There have been several plans for revival, including use for steam trains associated with the locomotive works at Tyseley and the most recent being for the station's reuse by Chiltern Railways. In the meantime, the station continues to survive. The freight area once provided on the west side of the station, after a period of being used for car parking, has been swept away by a new road that cuts into the railway arches under the station's former goods yard.

Below: 'Hall' class 4-6-0 No 5996 *Mytton Hall* is seen here accelerating past Moor Street station as it emerges from the Snow Hill Tunnel with the 5.45pm Snow Hill-Worcester, via Stratford-upon-Avon, train on 2 July 1960. The scrapping of this class of locomotive had already begun at this time. The tunnel seen here was closed in 1968, but was later to reopen. *M. Mensing*

Above: Moor Street with the 3.10pm to Henley-in-Arden, headed by 2-6-2T No 4173 on the left and the 3.20pm to Leamington Spa on the right, with 2-6-2T No 4112 in charge. This view was taken on 6 June 1957. The Moor Street freight shed, to the left of this view, remained well used at this time. *R. Darlaston*

Left: A three-car suburban DMU with No W50077 leading the 1.35pm local from Stratford-upon-Avon arriving at Moor Street on 27 February 1960. The signalbox and array of GWR lower quadrant signals in this view were to be swept away. *M. Mensing*

Lower left: Single-unit Gloucester-built DMU No W55004 waits to leave Moor Street, after being detached from the rear of the 1.30pm train from Leamington Spa on 31 March 1962. The movable metal traverser section of track, to the front of this view, was not taken out of use until 1967. *M. Mensing*

Right: In addition to suburban traffic, Moor Street was also originally built to operate excursion trains that could not be handled at Snow Hill. A Sunday service was provided for the Birmingham Super Prix, motor racing around the city streets. DMU Nos M55003, M59612 and M53100 are seen here forming the 08.12 Shirley-Moor Street, the first service of the day, on 24 August 1986.
R. Jones

Centre right: After closure in September 1987, the station at Moor Street remained unused and in a deteriorating condition. The site of the electrically driven, 60ft long traversers, which allowed locomotives of up to 'Castle' class size to transfer from one track to the other, can still be seen. Nature gradually reclaims unused railway facilities, even in a city centre, as this view taken in August 2001 shows. It is interesting to compare the growth of vegetation in this view with a similar view in *Lost Lines: Western* that was taken in 1993. Since this view was taken, the vegetation has been cut back and restoration undertaken. *Author's collection*

Lower right: Compare this scene with the activity in the first photograph in this chapter. This view of the derelict railway was taken in 1984, before a new Moor Street station was repositioned on the site of the former Moor Street relief lines, when the line was reopened into Snow Hill. A marker peg is the first indication of the reopening that would follow. It is of interest that the sleepers on this reopened line were salvaged from the closed Sheffield-Manchester Woodhead route.
E. Godward

⑥ Old New Street

The LNWR extended and altered the line from its cramped Curzon Street station to link into New Street and the passenger station opened in June 1854, in what was originally a rough part of Birmingham. Curzon Street, which had also been used by the Midland Railway since the closure of its terminus at Lawley Street in May 1851, closed at the same time, but was used by passenger excursions to Sutton Coldfield until May 1893 and as a freight depot.

New Street station was extended to provide the Midland Railway with its own platforms by 1885 and effectively became two stations separated by Queen's Drive. By 1893 additional approach tracks had been added to cope with increased use and from 1897 it became a joint station, but the different characters of the LNWR and MR sections were to remain until its demolition.

Many of the station buildings were of an imposing, high Victorian Barryesque style. Cowper designed the main LNWR side overall roof, which had a span of 209ft and a length of 840ft, but the train shed, facing the prevailing wind, acted on occasions as a wind tunnel. The overall roof was damaged during World War 2 and was removed in 1948, with individual asbestos awnings being provided over the ex-LNWR platforms, although the Midland side remained largely intact. A continued lack of maintenance gradually led the whole of the station into a poor state of repair and it became increasingly dirty and neglected. The Midland side was still gas lit into the 1960s.

In the 1960s the station employed around 600 staff, but passengers complained of the smell of the fish bay and the toilets. Consequently, although the current station is not to all tastes, there is little doubt that it represents some improvement over the earlier facilities. Very little of the original station remains, although an ex-LNWR plaque to those who were killed from the station during World War 1 can be found by the ticket booths, together with a few remains on the fringes of the station where original stores and bridge abutments endure.

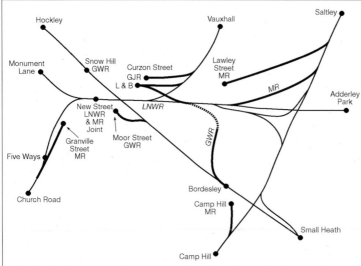

Above: The Queens Hotel at Birmingham New Street dated from 1854 and was subject to a number of extensions before its closure. It is seen here in the course of demolition in July 1966. The hotel was retained as long as possible and was the last major building to be demolished at New Street, closing on 31 December 1965, to make way for new development and station. The entrance to the original station was through the street level colonnades. The author took this view when, as a schoolboy, a first ever visit was made to Birmingham. *Author*

Right: Ex-LNWR 'Coal Tank' 0-6-2T No 58928 on duty at the south end of the ex-LNWR side of New Street station on 20 September 1950. Three hundred of these attractive late Victorian locomotives were built and the last survived until 1958.
P. B. Whitehouse

Below: A rare double-chimney 'Jubilee' class 4-6-0, No 45742 *Connaught*, based at Bushbury shed, just starting to move under the authority of the 'calling on' signal arm. Fowler Class 4MT 2-6-4T No 42345, one of the first of this wheel arrangement introduced by the LMS in 1927, waits at the opposite platform with a stopping train to Coventry, on the former Midland side of the station. This view was taken on Sunday, 13 September 1953. *E. D. Bruton*

Left: LMS 'Patriot' class 4-6-0 No 45505 *The Royal Army Ordnance Corps* waits to take over the 'Pines Express' at Platform 9 on 1 March 1958. The roster that this engine worked brought it to New Street at 12.53pm on a train from Liverpool and Manchester. It then crossed over to the Midland side of the station, as shown here. This whole class of locomotive was scrapped between 1960 and 1962.
M. Mensing

Below: BR Class 4 4-6-0 No 75009 leads BR Class 5 4-6-0 No 73016 with the 8am Newcastle-Cardiff train, arriving at New Street on 27 August 1960. Scrapping of both classes of locomotive began in 1964. The disparate nature of the old station building to the rear of this view is apparent. *Ian Allan Library*

Right: A three-car Cravens DMU waits to leave a cavernous New Street with the 3.15pm to Leicester on 12 July 1958. It can be seen that the ex-Midland side of the station was still gas lit at this time, although several gas lamps illuminating an entire platform could automatically be lit or extinguished at the same time. Train indicators, of the finger board variety, were also manually operated at this time. *M. Mensing*

Right: The sufferings of the area in World War 2 were immense. This view, taken on 7 July 1948 at Birmingham New Street, shows the demolition of the war-damaged roof and the construction of a temporary awning. This also shows the specially built demolition gantry. The work was all undertaken many years before the entire station was redeveloped. *BR*

Right: A few remnants of the old station endure. These former lamp room buildings were located on the ex-LNWR side of the station. How they survived such a radical rebuilding is not entirely clear, but they remain to this day and were viewed here in October 2001. *Author's collection*

7 The Harborne Express

Relatively few mainly suburban branch lines were built in the area, but the Harborne branch was an exception. It was also an exception in being one of the few lines so close to the centre of Birmingham to remain as a single line. In August 1874 the 2½-mile Harborne Railway opened. There were plans for extensions and connections to other railways, but these came to nothing and the line as built ran from Harborne Junction, off the Stour Valley line, to Harborne. However, a ½-mile freight-only line to a nearby brewery was opened in 1909. At one time a frequent weekday passenger service built up over the branch and in 1910 four trains left Harborne between 8am and 9am for the short trip to Birmingham. A suburb built up around the station at Harborne, the mock Tudor villas giving the area a rural character, and W. H. Auden of 'Night Mail' fame once lived here. Trains were run at midday so that workers in Birmingham could return home for lunch. The railway was worked by the LNWR, and turned in a profit, managing to remain independent until 1922.

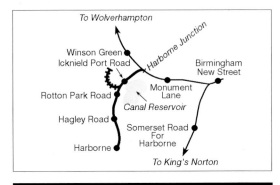

Below: For many years, Monument Lane shed provided most of the motive power for the Harborne branch. Here, a grimy ex-LNWR Webb 0-6-2T, based at Monument Lane, is seen with a freight working on the steeply graded branch in LMS days.
J. Mills

Right: Rotton Park Road station, taken before its closure to passengers in November 1934. New station buildings were provided here in 1902, together with a passing loop that created an island platform. However, after closure to passengers the station was not retained for goods and was subsequently demolished. *SLS*

Bottom: The Harborne branch timetable of services in April 1910.

At its peak, Harborne was the busiest commuter station to Birmingham and even the Midland Railway named its nearest station 'Somerset Road for Harborne', but tram and bus services cut into revenue . Joining the main Stour Valley line, near Birmingham New Street, it was also subject to delay. Passenger services were withdrawn from Icknield Port Road in May 1931 and ended over the entire branch in November 1934. There were attempts at a passenger revival, but these came to nothing.

Freight continued for much longer. Apart from general freight, and coal in particular, services provided materials for a toy company located close to the branch. As an aside, my very first clockwork toy locomotive came from here, the Chad Valley Toy Company. Mitchell & Butler's brewery at Cape Hill also provided much traffic for the branch until the firm transferred its freight to road transport in 1962. On occasions the branch was used to store carriages and special trains when the sidings at Monument Lane were full. A number of enthusiast specials also used the branch and in 1962 a DMU operated over the line for the first time. The final special was run by the Stephenson Locomotive Society in November 1963, and all remaining freight services ended shortly after. The special train was booked to capacity well before the event and at Harborne crowds came out to say a fond farewell to this attractive little branch.

All trace of former stations has gone and much of the freight branch to the brewery is difficult to follow, although it is possible to walk almost the entire length of the route from Harborne to where it once crossed the Birmingham Main Line Canal near Monument Lane. The lineside growth has been such that much of the walk now appears to be in a remote rural area, rather than in a great conurbation.

BIRMINGHAM and HARBORNE. — London and North Western.

(Harborne branch timetable, April 1910 — down and up services, times as printed.)

HARBORNE and BIRMINGHAM. — London and North Western.

(Harborne to Birmingham timetable, times as printed.)

NOTES.

e Except Saturdays.

† New Street Station; about ½ mile to Snow Hill Station (G.W.).

Left: A weedkilling train climbing the 1 in 66 grade in the Chad Valley on the Harborne branch in LMR days. During the last years of the branch, weedkilling was reduced and some sections of the track became more overgrown. *Ian Allan Library*

Left: A special passenger train was organised over the Harborne branch by the Stephenson Locomotive Society on 3 June 1950. 'Spruced up' Webb 2-4-2T No 46757 is seen at the overgrown but largely intact Harborne terminus, with the two-coach special train. The locomotive, from Walsall shed, was the last such engine to work over the branch. *E. Knight*

Below: The remains of the disused Harborne station in February 1966. The station canopy still survived at this time, although passenger services had ended in 1934. After this view was taken the site was subsequently cleared and redeveloped as a residential area. *A. Muckley*

Above: A view showing the removal of the remaining girders from the bridge that carried the Harborne branch over the Birmingham Main Line Canal near Harborne Junction, after final abandonment of the branch in 1964. Sulzer Type 2 (Class 24) No D5003 is seen in charge. In 1953, a number of freight wagons were derailed at this point and fell into the canal. *BR*

Right: The Harborne branch bridge abutment still remains today, looking almost like a submarine emerging in the Birmingham Main Line Canal when this view was taken, looking north, in August 2000. *Author*

Below: 1930s fares.

HARBORNE (Stafford).   117 miles.   Fares, 23/9a, 14/2s; Return, 47/6a, 28/4c.   From London as to Birmingham (New Street), thence 15 minutes, frequent service. Pop. 16,852.

Left: The old goods yard and weighbridge office at the former Hagley Road station, looking north in February 1966, after complete closure of the line. The weighbridge was being dismantled at this time. Nothing remains today, with the exception of the railway cottages beyond the fence. *A. Muckley*

Centre left: The site of the former Rotton Park Road station, looking north. In the centre of this view, which was taken in February 1966, the position of the former station's island platform can be clearly discerned. The site still remains, but is rather more overgrown than when this view was taken. *A. Muckley*

Below left: The largest brick bridge on the branch was this one near Harborne station. A slight subsidence threatened to result in the demolition of the bridge, but fortunately it still survives as the largest monument to the old railway. It is possible to walk from this bridge almost all the way to Monument Lane. This view was taken in August 2000. *Author*

Below: All the over bridges on the Harborne branch were of a similar design to this one and were built to accommodate only a single-track railway. Lineside growth is now considerable and the former railway acts as an attractive footpath for almost all its length. This view was taken in August 2000, near the site of the former Icknield Port Road station. After closure, the remaining stations on the branch were demolished. *Author*

⑧ Main Line Memories

In November 1854, the GWR opened a double-track, 10½-mile line from Birmingham Snow Hill to Priestfield, after which trains ran over the OWWR to Cannock Road Junction at Wolverhampton. It was originally a mixed gauge route, but the use of broad gauge was outlawed by the Gauge Act and, as a result, only standard gauge trains used the line after 1864.

Although the act effectively ended the dream of the GWR for a broad gauge line from London to the Mersey, the section between Birmingham Snow Hill and Wolverhampton Low Level became both a key artery in the area and also a section of the GWR's main line from London to Birkenhead.

There had been problems with some of the bridges on the line and Brunel had been forced to step in and strengthen these structures before the original route could be opened. Traffic grew considerably and by 1909 quadrupling work between Handsworth Junction and Birmingham had been undertaken. The main line could accommodate the largest of locomotives and the mighty 'King' class was able to use the route as far north as Wolverhampton. In addition to the main line expresses, services also developed from intermediate stations, with through summer services being provided from some of the larger stations to the West Country.

In the early days of Nationalisation the WR remained entrenched in the area and the main line operated largely as it had done under the GWR, but at Wednesbury the WR station became known as Central. Although the earlier railway companies had seen the GWR main line as a rival in the area, it suffered most when the railways were unified under BR. In 1963, the main line became part of the LMR and it seemed almost as if earlier rivalries still existed as the greatest closures came to ex-GWR lines when under the LMR administration. In reality it was primarily a result of Dr Beeching's plan at that time to cut out any seemingly duplicated routes.

Main line services were withdrawn in March 1967, with the ending of the Paddington-Birkenhead expresses and, after a fight, the remaining local services ceased in March 1972. The track was removed, although two sections remained for freight, from Smethwick Junction to the Handsworth & Smethwick cement terminal and from Wednesbury Town Junction to Bilston scrapyard, both sections being closed during the 1990s.

This once busy main line artery was closed and the roar of the main line expresses is just a memory, but it was not to be the end. Today Snow Hill-Smethwick Junction trains use part of the route, while the Midland Metro tramway uses most of the former main line with a frequency of service to intermediate stations that was never provided in the past.

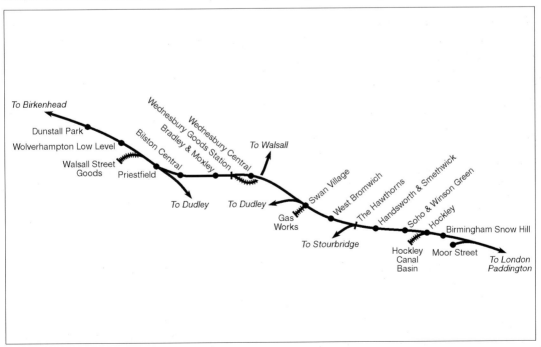

Left: GWR main line splendour. 'Star' class 4-6-0 No 4027 *King Henry* on an up Birkenhead express train, of GWR chocolate and cream coaches, at Handsworth Junction. The engine was renamed *Norwegian Monarch* in November 1927. *Ian Allan Library*

Centre left: 'King' class No 6011 *King James I* heads the 8.55am Birkenhead-Paddington express as it approaches Handsworth & Smethwick on Friday, 22 June 1956. This view was taken from the 11.45am Birmingham-Stourbridge train. *M. Walker*

Below: A Paddington-Portmadoc Festiniog Railway Society special train, headed by the preserved ex-GWR 4-4-0 No 3440 *City of Truro*, seen passing Dunstall Park on 30 March 1957. This locomotive held the world speed record of 102.3mph for a number of years. Dunstall Park station near Wolverhampton was opened in 1896 and served the nearby racecourse and Stafford Road Works. The station closed in 1968. Note the cast-iron station toilets next to the signalbox. *G. Bannister*

Above: 'Grange' class 4-6-0 No 6866 *Morfa Grange* on an up semi-fast passing Swan Village, on 3 August 1957. Before final closure, the original Swan Village gas-lit station buildings seen here were demolished and replaced by new buildings, which in turn were demolished on closure of the line.
M. Mensing

Below: Class 4300 2-6-0 No 6340 with the 4.35pm Stourbridge Junction-Birmingham Snow Hill, via Dudley, train arriving at West Bromwich station on 17 September 1958. This train then formed the 6.5pm Snow Hill-Leamington Spa service. The fine proportions of the station building were one of the very characteristic designs to be found along the Birmingham-Wolverhampton main line. The imposing buildings seen to the rear of this view were demolished after closure. *M. Mensing*

Left: The main line was an important freight artery. BR Standard Class 9F 2-10-0 No 92127 enters Bilston Central with a westbound steel freight train in March 1966. BR added Central to the station's name in 1950. When this view was taken, it was the twilight years for all steam locomotives in the area and the '9F' seen here was withdrawn the following year. *A. Muckley*

Left: A freight train, hauled by 'Black 5' 4-6-0 No 44865, pulls into Hockley goods depot sidings, as seen from Hockley station looking east, in March 1966. Access to this major GWR freight yard was improved with the quadrupling of lines out of Snow Hill. The yard contained a 25-ton crane, the largest in the Birmingham area. All freight ended in 1971. *A. Muckley*

Left: The Hawthorns Halt opened in December 1932 to serve West Bromwich Albion football ground. In this view, Class 5101 2-6-2T No 4110 is seen heading an empty stock football special from the Stourbridge line on 25 March 1961. This train was one of several local excursions run in connection with a West Bromwich Albion v Everton football match on that day. The halt closed in 1968 but the site is served by the Midland Metro. *M. Mensing*

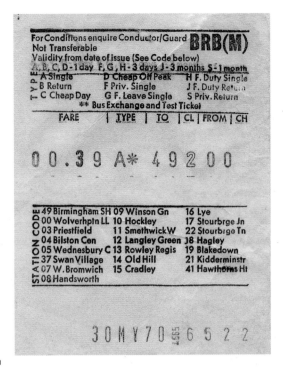

Below: Stanier '8F' 2-8-0 No 48543 passes Handsworth & Smethwick with an up freight on 31 December 1964. A three-car DMU leaves the station in the background, on a down local. *J. Cooper-Smith*

Left: Main line diesels began to replace steam. Here we see WR Swindon-built 'Western' class 2,700hp diesel-hydraulic No D1006 *Western Stalwart* on an up 'Cambrian Coast Express', passing Soho & Winson Green station on 18 August 1962. *M. Mensing*

Left: Brush Type 4 No D1696 heads the 8.10am Shrewsbury-Paddington train, climbing from Swan Village to West Bromwich on Sunday, 26 April 1964. *M. Mensing*

Right: The subway at Hockley station in March 1966. The classic GWR sign with its hand pointing 'To up and down platforms' would probably be little understood by the general travelling public today. The dirty white-glazed bricks and the ruinous roof added to an air of desolation. Almost all the stations on this former main line became very run down before closure and this did little to encourage passenger numbers.
A. Muckley

Left: A three-car Birmingham suburban DMU, with 'cat's whiskers' front markings, is seen here on a Wellington-Leamington Spa train entering the imposing stone-dressed Wednesbury Central station on 29 May 1960. Some modernisation of the station's platform lamps had been undertaken at this time. This remains an industrial area, although not so intense as when this view was taken. *R. C. Riley*

Right: Soho & Winson Green station, looking towards Wolverhampton in March 1966. One of the platform buildings had been renewed at this time, but unlike some other stations on the line, gas remained as platform lighting. The 'Soho &' of the station's name had been painted out in order to try to capitalise on Winson Green traffic after closure of Winson Green station on the Stour Valley line in 1957. *A. Muckley*

Centre right: Little modernisation had been undertaken to this ex-GWR station when this view of Hockley was taken in March 1966. The bands of blue and white bricks distinguished the building, but it was closed in 1972 and subsequently demolished. *A. Muckley*

Right: The last few years of this former main line saw a great deal of dereliction develop at the intermediate stations, which had become unstaffed halts in May 1969. Here, 'Bubblecar' No W55004 is seen at Priestfield, on 19 December 1969, with the 13.50 Saturdays-only Wolverhampton Low Level-Birmingham Snow Hill service. The single units were introduced in 1968 as a result of poor patronage on the line. Closure came to all the remaining halts in 1972. *N. Griffiths*

⑨ I Want To Go To Birmingham

The Black Country was littered with railway junctions. Catching the correct train on the correct platform could confuse the unsuspecting traveller as the famous words by Le Brunn suggest:

'Oh! Mr Porter, what shall I do?
I want to go to Birmingham
And they're taking me on to Crewe.'

Such junctions often witnessed bursts of frantic activity as trains made tight connections, but those trains, not always running to time, could on occasions lead to general passenger confusion. Some junctions were also to witness intrigue, mystery and even crime as all of life passed onto their platforms and over their tracks. Advertised connections were sometimes not made at all and there was the famous excuse when a GWR employee, questioned as to why a connecting train had not been held, responded that 'The GWR has its reasons.' Take this extract, from the tale *Dead on Time* relating to Priestfield in the heart of the Black Country:

'Having been satisfied with the arrangements to protect the special train, I made my way to a deserted platform at Priestfield, never anyone to ask when you need them, I thought. It was a late summer's afternoon and I enjoyed the sun through the haze. A gas light burnt aimlessly on one of the platforms as a Birkenhead express roared through, hauled by a very handsome looking engine called *King James I*. Those still eating in the restaurant car looked out blankly onto the empty platform. No sooner had the express gone by than a freight engine from the branch clanked onto the main line. My local to Snow Hill was the next arrival; the train seemed a little early, what good fortune I thought. I sank into the horsehair moquette-covered seat of an empty compartment. It would have been very agreeable to lower the window, because although the heating handle was in the 'off' position there was that distinctive smell and warmth to the steam-heated compartment. Nevertheless, I had to keep the window strap tight to prevent smoke entering the compartment as the train gathered speed past the rows of back-to-back houses and grimy trackside works. I mused on the map of GWR destinations, six stations to Birmingham, when a porter shouted 'Wolverhampton, Wolverhampton Low Level'.

Priestfield is no longer a junction, although the slick Midland Metro now uses the site. Furthermore the ghosts of such past junctions can be brought to life if you take the junction at Kidderminster for the preserved Severn Valley Railway.

Left: 'King' class 4-6-0 No 6026 *King John* on the 2.35pm Birkenhead-Paddington service, taking the Birmingham line past a gas-lit Priestfield station, on 30 April 1960. *M. Mensing*

Right: Class 4300 2-6-0 No 7317 on a down freight, coming off the Birmingham line at Priestfield on 30 April 1960. The lines in the foreground lead to Stourbridge Junction, via Dudley. *M. Mensing*

Right: Class 5101 2-6-2T No 5151 on the 5.27pm Stourbridge Junction-Wolverhampton Low Level service, leaving Priestfield station on 30 April 1960. *M. Mensing*

Below: Priestfield station, seen from the Wolverhampton direction, in March 1966. The platforms straight ahead served Dudley, those curving off to the left serving Birmingham. The section of line between Priestfield and Dudley was taken out of use in 1967 and that to Birmingham in 1973. All the tracks here were subsequently lifted. *A. Muckley*

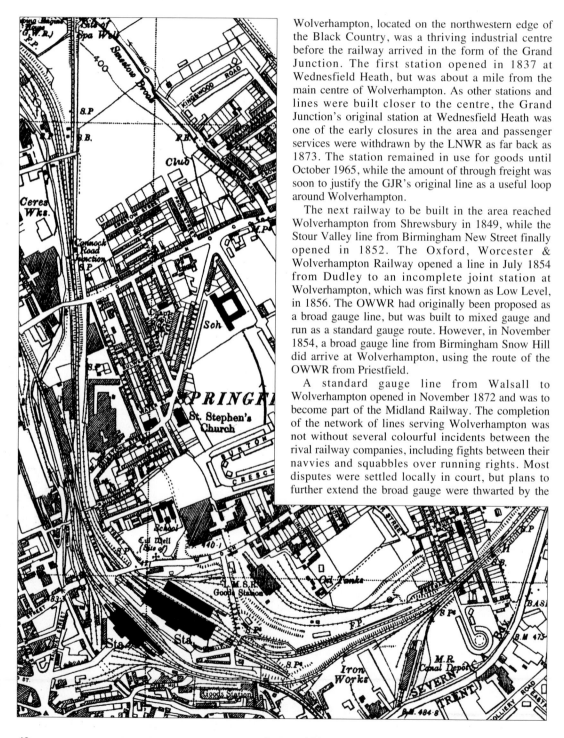

Wolverhampton, located on the northwestern edge of the Black Country, was a thriving industrial centre before the railway arrived in the form of the Grand Junction. The first station opened in 1837 at Wednesfield Heath, but was about a mile from the main centre of Wolverhampton. As other stations and lines were built closer to the centre, the Grand Junction's original station at Wednesfield Heath was one of the early closures in the area and passenger services were withdrawn by the LNWR as far back as 1873. The station remained in use for goods until October 1965, while the amount of through freight was soon to justify the GJR's original line as a useful loop around Wolverhampton.

The next railway to be built in the area reached Wolverhampton from Shrewsbury in 1849, while the Stour Valley line from Birmingham New Street finally opened in 1852. The Oxford, Worcester & Wolverhampton Railway opened a line in July 1854 from Dudley to an incomplete joint station at Wolverhampton, which was first known as Low Level, in 1856. The OWWR had originally been proposed as a broad gauge line, but was built to mixed gauge and run as a standard gauge route. However, in November 1854, a broad gauge line from Birmingham Snow Hill did arrive at Wolverhampton, using the route of the OWWR from Priestfield.

A standard gauge line from Walsall to Wolverhampton opened in November 1872 and was to become part of the Midland Railway. The completion of the network of lines serving Wolverhampton was not without several colourful incidents between the rival railway companies, including fights between their navvies and squabbles over running rights. Most disputes were settled locally in court, but plans to further extend the broad gauge were thwarted by the

Gauge Act, which forbade any broad gauge extension northward, beyond Wolverhampton. With the broad gauge being forced to end at Wolverhampton, the transhipment between the gauges made the town one of particular importance on the GWR.

The status of Wolverhampton was reinforced by the GWR when it took over Stafford Road Works and the first express passenger locomotive was produced there in 1858. Broad gauge was gradually withdrawn southwards from Wolverhampton and from November 1864 all passenger trains were restricted to standard gauge, with full conversion from broad gauge being completed by 1869. Stafford Road Works declined in importance with the removal of 7ft gauge in the area. Locomotive construction was later transferred to Swindon, but the works remained important for repairs and other projects until 1964 when dieselisation and contraction of the network finally resulted in its closure.

The development of the railways at Wolverhampton led to two stations being built. The GWR Low Level station was located below the LNWR High Level

Opposite Left: A map of the High and Low Level stations and goods yards at Wolverhampton in 1938. *Crown Copyright*

Right: A passage known as the Colonnades led from the ex-LNWR High Level station at Wolverhampton to the ex-GWR Low Level station. Although the pedestrian link was no longer required between the two stations, the passageway remained in use when this view was taken of the Low Level station in August 2000. The distinctive white roofs of the platform canopies, which replaced Brunel's original overall roof, were still apparent. *Author*

Right: Wolverhampton Low Level station on 16 June 1957. GWR 4-4-0 No 3440 *City of Truro* is seen at the head of a Stephenson Locomotive Society excursion to Swindon Works. The service train to Stourbridge Junction, Kidderminster and Worcester stands in the bay with 2-6-2T No 5106 in charge. *G. Bannister*

Above: 'Castle' class 4-6-0 No 5047 *Earl of Dartmouth* leaves Wolverhampton Low Level on Saturday, 12 September 1959 with the 11.10am Paddington-Birkenhead train. Note the pole for overhead wires on the Wednesbury Road bridge for Wolverhampton's trolleybuses. *M. Mensing*

Left: The 2.10pm to Stourbridge Junction, via Dudley, train waits to leave Wolverhampton Low Level on Whit Monday, 11 June 1962 behind 'Castle' class 4-6-0 No 5070 *Sir Daniel Gooch*. The engine came off the up 'Cambrian Coast Express'. The high wall, backing the platform canopy, was retained after the original overall roof was demolished in 1934. *M. Mensing*

Right: Swindon-built 2,700hp 'Western' class diesel-hydraulic No D1000 *Western Enterprise*, in distinctive desert sand livery, is seen here on the 11.50am train from Stourbridge Junction, via Dudley, drawing out after arrival at Wolverhampton Low Level on 11 June 1962, on a crew-training run. This local service ceased at the end of the following month.
M. Mensing

Right: Class 5700 0-6-0PT No 3778 at Wolverhampton Low Level, shunting stock, including a refreshment car, on to the rear of the 8.50am Birkenhead-Paddington service on 11 June 1962. High Level station in the background retained its overall roof when this view, to the north of the stations, was taken.
M. Mensing

Right: Class 5700 0-6-0PTs Nos 9630 and 9610 wait outside Wolverhampton Low Level to let a Birmingham-bound DMU pass, before they leave for Stratford-upon-Avon with the Stephenson Locomotive Society's special train, 'Farewell to the GWR Pannier Tanks', on 11 September 1966.
Brian Stephenson

Left: A view in August 2000, showing the once busy area of track to the north of Wolverhampton Low Level. The lines to the north of the station were last used by freight trains in 1969. After a period of car storage the former main line had become an overgrown wasteland when this view was taken. *Author*

station. The substantial GWR station was provided with two through platforms, three bays and an overall roof. The roof became unsafe and was demolished in 1933, but the station survived World War 2 and remained an important stop on the London-Birkenhead route.

In March 1967, the through London-Birkenhead trains were discontinued and only local services to Shrewsbury and Snow Hill remained. In May 1970, the Low Level station became a parcel depot, although a platform was retained for the remaining Snow Hill service until this also ended in March 1972. The station closed to rail traffic in 1981, but the buildings were listed in 1986.

In a final twist in the history of railways in the area, the original buildings of the LNWR station have been demolished, although the station remains open. On the other hand, the buildings of the closed GWR station largely remain and are still linked to the ex-LNWR station, some 30ft above, by a now rather uninviting white-tiled subway and colonnaded passage.

In 2002, the former GWR station remained in an unused condition and it has to be said that the once proud presence of the GWR in the area is very much reduced. Yet today, you can travel through the streets of the city of Wolverhampton once again by tram. Who would have believed this in 1967, so who knows what the future may bring?

Left: The former through roads at Wolverhampton Low Level are now sidings by the time of this 1976 scene, the station having become a parcels concentration depot in 1970. This view was taken from the site of the demolished south box. All operational railway use of the depot and station ended in June 1981. *Ian Allan Library*

Left: Final closure of the parcels depot at Wolverhampton Low Level came in 1981. The station has seen little use since 1985 and the buildings are in an ever-deteriorating condition. The track still remains between the platforms, and a parcels van which was marooned on the site when links to the station were severed had been subject to an arson attack when this view was taken in January 2002. *Author*

11 All Stations to Brettell Lane

The OWWR opened a standard gauge line from Kingswinford South Junction on the Stourbridge-Dudley line to the Bromley canal basin in November 1858. By the 1860s this had been extended to serve the Earl of Dudley's Pensnett Railway. Much later, authorisation for a link northwards to Dunstall Park near Oxley sidings was granted, but work on the route was disrupted because of World War 1 and it was not until 1919 that building work was fully under way. As it turned out, construction was further delayed because of mining subsidence in the area and thus it was that the 12-mile line between Oxley and Baggeridge Junction only finally opened to freight in January 1925, and to passengers in May of that year.

The delays meant that it was one of the last major railway lines to be built in the area and even as the route was opening, other branch lines in the vicinity were closing. The route was single track north of Gornal Halt, but a passing loop was provided at Wombourn.

Towns and villages along the route were expanding, but the line as built was only part of a wider scheme. The route ran tangentially to Wolverhampton and with stations such as Wombourn located on the edge of the town, direct bus services into Wolverhampton from the main settlements soon ate into railway revenue. Steam railmotors were used and halts were provided at Brockmoor, Bromley, Pensnett, Gornal, Penn and Compton, in addition to the stations at Himley, Wombourn and Tettenhall, in a bid to attract more passengers. It was all to no avail: limited numbers used the line and passenger services were withdrawn in October 1932, after just seven years.

As it turned out, the line developed as an important route for freight. The link provided a useful bypass around Wolverhampton for north-south freight trains, and a triangular junction at Oxley allowed flexibility of traffic movements. The route also proved useful for freight movements during World War 2. Use declined after the war and the last sections of the single line, which had become part of the LMR, closed between Oxley North Junction as far as Baggeridge Junction in February 1965. The section south from Baggeridge Junction to Pensnett Junction closed in April 1968, together with Baggeridge Colliery.

On closure, the line was at first abandoned and the station buildings fell into a state of considerable disrepair, but fortunately local authorities in the area saw the recreation potential of the closed line. The route runs out from the urban area of Wolverhampton into the countryside and much of the former line is now used as a public footpath. The main passenger station building at Wombourn (as spelt by the GWR) is used as a café, while the buildings at Tettenhall station remain in their original GWR glory. Bridges and structures on the line have also been restored. Although a lost line, the route itself remains intact and is well used by ramblers and cyclists. The section of line between Kingswinford Junction and Pensnett is still in situ, but the railway is currently unused.

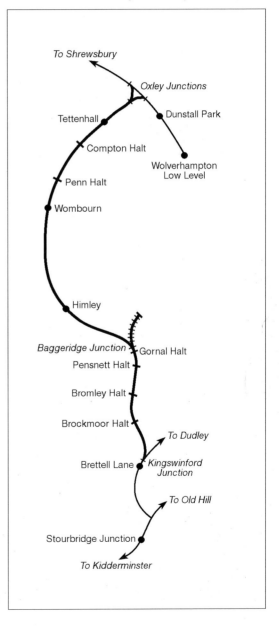

Above: Oxley Branch Junction at Wolverhampton. The Oxley Sidings-Baggeridge Junction local freight, with an 0-6-0PT in charge, waits for BR Standard Class 4 4-6-0 No 75024 to clear the single line from Wombourn, with an empty ballast train to Oswestry on 24 April 1957. Today, all trace of the tracks at this junction has gone. *G. Bannister*

Left: Tettenhall station is seen in this view in 1949. The second platform, which was provided in anticipation of passenger traffic over the line, including to the nearby racecourse, was used in July 1937 to serve the Royal Agricultural Society's Royal Show. All the ex-GWR railway buildings in this view still survive. *Ian Allan Library*

Right: Tettenhall station today. It is now part of a Ranger station on a long-distance footpath which uses the route of the old railway. This view of the well-preserved building was taken in August 2001. *Author*

Right: The goods shed and office still survive at Tettenhall and the GWR sign, partly painted out by BR, also endures. These buildings were the last traditional set of GWR buildings to be constructed in this country and fortunately still survive relatively unchanged. This view was taken in August 2001. *Author*

Below: The view looking northwards over rolling countryside from the overbridge near Wombourn station on 4 September 1954. The water crane and single-line loop formation are both apparent. Some land, for a possible doubling of the line, was purchased and many bridges on the route were built with the potential to accommodate double tracks, should this have been required. *D. Kelk*

Above: Wombourn station on 4 September 1954. The station remained in use for freight for many years after its closure to passengers in 1932. The view here shows the signalbox and the single-line token equipment. The large water tank is visible to the right of this view. The station was used during World War 2 to take wounded solders to Wolverhampton's New Cross Hospital. *Ian Allan Library*

Centre left: Wombourn station in August 2001. A Stephenson Locomotive Society special was the last passenger train to call at the station, in June 1964, and the last freight train ran through a year later. Note that Wombourne, as now spelt with an 'e', was never used as such by the GWR. The passenger building, when this view was taken, was used as a café and visitor centre on the railway walk. The walk uses much of the former railway from Oxley to Pensnett. *Author*

Lower left: One of the platform edges still survives at Wombourn and it is clear how the vegetation has grown over the years since the track was removed by 1968. The main ex-GWR passenger station building remains largely unchanged from earlier views although after passenger closure, all the station footbridges were removed on the line. This view was taken in August 2001. *Author*

Above: Class 5700 0-6-0PT No 8718 climbs towards Brettell Lane (as spelt by the GWR), with a lengthy Stourbridge-Wolverhampton goods train on 1 July 1966. The branch to Wombourn divided from the main Stourbridge-Wolverhampton line at Kingswinford Junction, a little further along the line from this view. *S. Cotton*

12 The GWR That Never Was

A number of plans by the GWR never came to fruition. In Birmingham, Brunel was obliged to provide a ¼-mile link from his mixed gauge GWR line to the LNWR line close to New Street in order to reach Curzon Street. As a result, in 1853 work was started on the substantial main line Duddeston Viaduct by the GWR. However, once work was well under way, the LNWR decided not to allow the GWR to complete the section on its land, as it feared the link would result in the use of its New Street station by the GWR. Consequently, the substantial double track blue engineering brick viaduct still snakes its way around the south of the city centre, ending within sight of the former LNWR main line. Although part of the viaduct was used as a siding and one of the arches as a huge advert for Bordesley Cattle station, it never saw regular passenger trains and remains one of the largest monuments to a GWR route that never was in the area.

The GWR had plans for a new hotel at Birmingham Snow Hill. The proposed 1930s ultra modern design was in complete contrast to the ornate, highly decorated design of the original hotel at Snow Hill that had been purchased by the GWR in 1906. Whether the new building would have done anything to save the station is doubtful, but the imposing new building may have been less likely to have been demolished than the original hotel. As it turned out, plans for the hotel were hit by the recessionary years of the 1930s, while World War 2 finally put paid to the idea.

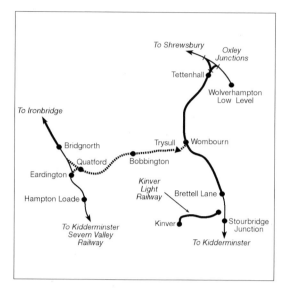

While the GWR had consolidated its position to the southeast of Birmingham, it had authorisation for a number of new lines to the northwest of the city. The line via Wombourn was the most ambitious and was outlined in the previous chapter. A proposed extension westwards never came to fruition. Authorisation was obtained for a junction off the line at Wombourn and the proposed single line would

Left: Part of the substantial blue engineering brick-built Duddeston Viaduct, which snakes its way around the southern part of Birmingham from the main GWR line almost to the main LNWR line. Although the viaduct never served its intended main line railway purpose, as is usual in urban areas, good use has been made of the arches. This view was taken in August 2000 and shows that most of the structure still remains, in spite of about 150 years of no real railway use. *Author*

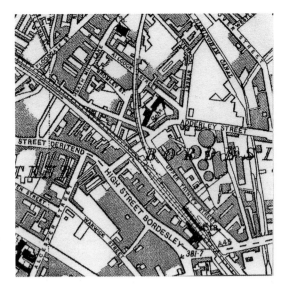

have run westwards near Bobbington and Quatford. It would have bridged the River Severn to join the Severn Valley line to the south of Bridgnorth, with a three-way junction to provide flexibility of operation. The line would have reduced the rail distances from Bridgnorth and Ironbridge to Wolverhampton considerably and run through attractive rolling countryside.

The line was surveyed, but bus competition, including a direct route from Bridgnorth to Wolverhampton started by the GWR in 1904 and transferred to Wolverhampton Corporation in 1923, saw off the rail project. Another idea tentatively considered, for a link to Kinver, was also dropped. Judging by the closure of the lines that the proposed railways were to connect with, the judgement to abandon the schemes was arguably sensible. Although none of the plans of the GWR mentioned here came into being, the company's entrepreneurial ambitions to expand in the area are to be applauded.

Above: A map of the Duddeston Viaduct at Bordesley station in 1928. *Crown Copyright*

Right: Although never employed for its original main line purpose, part of the viaduct was used as a goods siding and this arch at Bordesley at least provided the GWR with a huge advert for its Bordesley Cattle station, which developed after Moor Street goods depot opened in 1914. The faded white paint still survived in 2001, when this view was taken, more than 50 years after the GWR itself was no more. *Author*

Right: An elevation of the proposed Great Western Hotel in Birmingham, with its six floors and central ventilation shaft from Snow Hill station below. The plans were first revealed in 1939, but World War 2 intervened to thwart the project. This building would have replaced the original hotel and provided Birmingham with an impressive new landmark. Plans for office development over the current station reinforce the prime location of this site. *Ian Allan Library*

Above left: Had the GWR plans for a link to Bridgnorth gone ahead, Tettenhall station would have been a stop on a direct train service that struck out westwards from Wombourn to Eardington near Bridgnorth. This view was taken in August 2001 and shows the surviving station building in Valley Park. *Author*

Above: This is a view of the closed single line near Wombourn, not too far from where a junction would have struck off westwards to the Severn Valley line. The proposed route would have run through attractive countryside, as this view taken in August 2001 shows. No doubt the GWR would have hoped for suburban development along the proposed route and had this line come to fruition it may have changed the attractive rural landscape in parts of this area. *Author*

Lower left: Eardington Halt near Bridgnorth on 25 August 1963. Had the link to Wombourn been built, trains to Wolverhampton Low Level may have branched off the Severn Valley Railway at a three-way junction near here. A GWR service that never was, but the line remains open here and, courtesy of the Severn Valley Railway, provides a glimpse of the GWR that still is! *A. Muckley*

13 Great Works

Although this was a major industrial and railway area, a relatively limited number of steam locomotives was produced here, compared with some other parts of the country. Foster, Rastrick & Co built early locomotives at Stourbridge and *The Stourbridge Lion* was the first locomotive to be exported to America, where it worked well but was too heavy for the track and ended up driving machinery. The Horseley Iron Works at Tipton also built a few early locomotives. The Earl of Dudley established locomotive building at Dudley in about 1870 and a limited number of locomotives was built until the works closed in 1924. Stafford Road Works at Wolverhampton first began the construction of locomotives for the GWR in 1859 and by 1908, when all locomotive building was transferred to Swindon, 800 locomotives had been built. Locomotive repairs continued at the factory and the last Wolverhampton-built locomotive remained in service until 1963, with the works closing the following year.

Right: Continuing a theme of the last chapter, it was buses that put paid to a number of railway schemes in the area and led to the closure of some lines. The area became a centre for the manufacture of components and complete vehicles and this GWR all-weather coach was built with bodywork by John Buckingham Ltd of Birmingham. This view was taken in May 1929. *Ian Allan Library*

Right: Stafford Road Works at Wolverhampton was originally established by the Shrewsbury & Birmingham Railway in 1849, but soon became part of the GWR. In 1929 the GWR took advantage of a government public works programme to expand the works. This view shows the machine section and engine erecting shop after expansion work was completed on 27 July 1932. Once engine building was transferred to Swindon, in 1908, the works did not build locomotives but remained important for heavy repairs and maintenance. *Ian Allan Library*

Above: 'Manor' class 4-6-0 No 7819 *Hinton Manor* was being overhauled at Stafford Road Works, Wolverhampton, on 24 March 1957. At its peak over 1,500 were employed at the works. The replacement of steam by fewer diesel and electric locomotives heralded the demise of the works and it closed in June 1964, ending over one hundred years of engine construction and maintenance at Wolverhampton. *M. Hale*

Left: The distinctive plaque from E. C. & J. Keay Ltd. The firm was responsible for a range of railway equipment, from signals to the metalwork for the roof of Snow Hill station. This plaque was seen at the Birmingham Railway Museum at Tyseley in the summer of 2001. *Author's collection*

It was the construction of other railway equipment, and rolling stock in particular, which more heavily involved the area. For example, E. C. & J. Keay Ltd made all forms of signalling and metalwork at Darlaston. Other forms of railway equipment were made at mostly rail-connected works in the area, ranging from axleboxes and couplings to railway lamps.

Braithwaite & Kirk were established in 1884 at West Bromwich. They entered the Indian market in 1891 supplying a railway footbridge and rapidly developed the business, building some of the most impressive railway structures in the subcontinent. On a smaller scale, Bulpitt & Sons and G. Polkey Ltd, both of Birmingham, made lamps for many railways.

Of the closed rolling stock works, that of the Birmingham Railway Carriage & Wagon Co Ltd (BRCW) was the most well known and its factory was located west of Handsworth & Smethwick station. It was established in 1854 and developed exports to Africa, Europe and Australia. For the home market over

700 coaches and almost 120 DMUs, together with more than 200 Class 26, 27 and 33 diesel-electric locomotives, were built at the works for BR. The company also supplied parts for a prototype lightweight diesel locomotive, painted in white and named *Lion* (illustrated in Chapter 3). The distinctive design had some problems, but undoubtedly did form the basis of the successful Type 4 locomotive. Indeed, the original engine block was transferred to a Type 4 and remained in use until 2000. However, no orders for the new locomotive were forthcoming and as a consequence the factory closed in 1963 with the loss of 7,000 jobs.

The part played by railway works in the area during World War 2 should not be forgotten. Production was switched from rolling stock to aid the war effort and everything from Spitfire aircraft parts to tanks were built at the railway factories. Railway equipment ranging from high-tech trains to guard's whistles are still made in the area.

Right: A BR(W) hand lamp made in Birmingham by G. Polkey Ltd. It was of very similar design to those produced by the GWR and displays an early reluctance by the WR to conform to the new BR standardised image after Nationalisation. *Author*

Below: A map showing the despoiled and heavily industrialised landscape, at the Staffordshire Steel & Ingot Iron Works at Spring Vale, Bilston, in 1928. The works had both standard and 2ft gauge lines. The works generated much freight traffic for the railways in the area, but closed in 1979. *Crown Copyright*

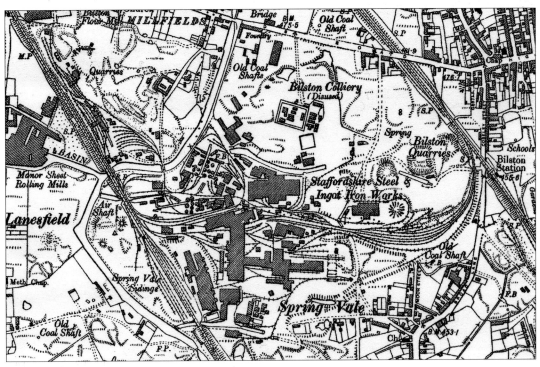

Above: Mobile showrooms: a train sponsored by Carpet Trades Limited provides great interest at Birmingham Snow Hill. The train toured the country in the mid-1960s and is seen here headed by preserved LNER 'K4' class 2-6-0 No 3442 *The Great Marquess*, an unusual visitor to the ex-GWR lines in the area at this time. *Ian Allan Library*

Left: Birmingham developed as a centre for exhibitions and trade fairs. Here, two locomotives, a Leeds-built Fowler 150hp diesel shunter and a Fowler Marshall 40hp narrow gauge diesel, are on display at the British Industries Fair that was held in May 1949. *Ian Allan Library*

14 Joint Line to Halesowen

Halesowen developed during the Industrial Revolution into a significant Black Country settlement. The GWR opened the first 1½-mile single line to the town from Old Hill in March 1878.

The second line to reach the town, was a six-mile link provided by the Halesowen Railway that ran from the Midland main line and opened in September 1883. There were difficulties of construction due to mining

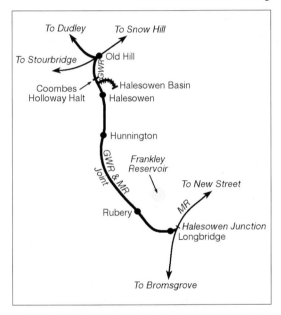

subsidence in the area and it was also a single line throughout, with stations in addition to Halesowen at Hunnington, Frankley and Rubery, and from 1915, at Longbridge. The two lines linked at Halesowen, to form a through freight route between the GWR to the north and the MR to the south. A freight-only line opened to the Halesowen Basin on the Dudley Canal in 1902.

In 1906, after bankruptcy, the former Halesowen Railway was vested jointly in the Great Western and Midland (later LMS) railways. The main passenger flows were to Dudley, but the necessity to change at Old Hill hardly encouraged their development. The southern part of the line travelled though attractive countryside and at Rubery connections could be made with trams that provided links to the Lickey Hills. As a result a tourist trade developed there. Nevertheless, freight was the principal use of the line: a steel works at Halesowen, the Blue Bird Toffee factory at Hunnington and, for a time, a one-mile link to Frankley Reservoir, all provided traffic. Yet it was the Austin works at Longbridge that came to dominate traffic over the line. The first siding to the works opened in 1915 and a platform for workers was opened in the same year.

The southern section of line included the slender and attractive metal viaduct at Dowery Dell near Hunnington. The viaduct necessitated a weight restriction on the route and resulted in elderly MR Kirtley 0-6-0s being retained for freight use on the line when all others in their class had been scrapped,

Right: The last passenger services to use the line were workmen's trains. Here, the weekdays-only Old Hill-Longbridge train, which was not advertised in the public timetables, is seen headed by Class 7400 0-6-0PT No 7435 alongside the Old Hill-Dudley ex-GWR railcar in May 1950. The workmen's service of two trains each way ran for the benefit of the Austin car workers with increasingly antiquated stock until services ended in September 1958. Old Hill remains open, but is much remodelled and almost all traces of the branches that once ran from the passenger station have gone.
P. B. Whitehouse

Left: Because of weight restrictions imposed over Dowery Dell Viaduct, older and lighter locomotives were used on the branch after they had been withdrawn from service elsewhere. Ex-MR Kirtley curved framed 0-6-0 No 22846 is seen at Halesowen in September 1949. Even at this time these engines only rarely worked the branch, as some inside-framed ex-MR '2Fs' were stationed at Brownhills for use on the line. *P. B. Whitehouse*

although heavier MR Johnson 0-6-0s were used after 1944.

In spite of some through trains to Birmingham New Street, Halesowen lost its regular public passenger trains to Northfield in April 1919. The remaining route to Old Hill provided a frequent service by using steam railmotors and a halt was added in 1905 called Coombes Holloway, but this line was to close to passengers in December 1927, although unadvertised workmen's passenger trains ran from Old Hill to Longbridge until September 1958. There was also a service to Longbridge from Birmingham and this was

Above: A Longbridge-Halesowen freight approaches the double Rubery down distant signal at 7.40pm on 22 May 1957, hauled by ex-MR Johnson 0-6-0 No 58167. The crossing keeper operated one arm of the signal and the signalman the other. The rural setting of much of this line is apparent from this view. *Ian Allan Library*

Above: Freight use of the line remained relatively buoyant until closure. Two 0-6-0PTs, Nos 3619 and 4646, are seen during shunting operations at Halesowen Canal Basin Junction on 8 September 1966. A steeply curving freight branch to the north of Halesowen station led to the canal basin. Today, the canal remains, but there is little trace of the railway at Halesowen. *J. Hunt*

Right: Class 5700 0-6-0PT No 9774 banks the afternoon Halesowen-Stourbridge Junction freight up the gradient out of Halesowen. No 3619 heads the train which was taken on from Old Hill by No 9774. This view of the attractive countryside, through which much of the line ran, was taken on 8 September 1966. *J. Hunt*

Below: The 660ft-long Dowery Dell Viaduct near Hunnington was a metal trestle viaduct which was unique in the area and is seen here with an Ivatt Class 2 2-6-0 heading a freight train passing 100ft overhead. The single-line viaduct had a weight restriction that limited the classes of locomotives that could use the branch. The view here was taken in June 1962. In common with many metal viaducts, it was demolished for its scrap value in 1965 after this section of line closed. *D. Walters*

advertised by a footnote to the main timetable until this service ceased in 1960. Freight ended between Halesowen and Rubery in January 1964 and from Rubery to Longbridge in July of that year. The Halesowen canal link and remaining freight line to Old Hill closed in October 1969.

After closure the metal viaduct at Dowery Dell was demolished and sold for scrap. Little now survives at Halesowen, but at Longbridge a section of the branch, including the Halesowen Junction name on the former Midland main line, remains in use to the MG Rover factory. The former passenger station buildings at Longbridge, which have been replaced by a new station on the main line, also remained in 2002. At Hunnington the station building still exists, while the single-line tunnel at Hayden Hill also survives, although heavily overgrown and sealed at its southern portal.

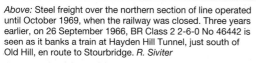

Above: Steel freight over the northern section of line operated until October 1969, when the railway was closed. Three years earlier, on 26 September 1966, BR Class 2 2-6-0 No 46442 is seen as it banks a train at Hayden Hill Tunnel, just south of Old Hill, en route to Stourbridge. *R. Siviter*

Above: The distorted tunnel portal, a result of mining subsidence, can be seen from this view of the south end of Hayden Hill Tunnel, looking towards Halesowen in June 1966. Note the overgrown track. Both tunnel portals remain in situ, although now much more heavily overgrown, and an earth mound has sealed the southern portal shown here. *A. Muckley*

Left: Halesowen station, looking north. The station had remained largely unchanged for many years when this view was taken in February 1966. After closure to regular passengers the footbridge and platform canopy on the signalbox side were removed. The station remained gas lit almost until the final workmen's trains ended in 1958. *A. Muckley*

Right: Ex-GWR 0-6-0PT No 9614 is seen shunting at an increasingly overgrown Halesowen, looking towards Rubery in June 1966. When this view was taken, the station canopy had recently been removed and the wooden remains lie on the platform. *A. Muckley*

Right: Class 5700 0-6-0PT No 9630 tops up with water, with a leaky hose, at Halesowen on 11 September 1966. The locomotive was on the Stephenson Locomotive Society's 'Farewell to the GWR Pannier Tanks' railtour which travelled over the line. *R. Ward*

Right: A Birmingham University Transport Society DMU special train at Halesowen, which at this time, was the terminus of the freight-only section from Old Hill. This view was taken on 2 March 1968 when much of interest still survived. No remains of Halesowen station can be found today. *A. Muckley*

Left: The substantial passenger station building at Hunnington still survived, but in a disused condition when this view was taken in February 1966. The platform lamps also remained, although the last advertised passenger services ran in 1919. Workmen's trains continued after that time, until 1958. *A. Muckley*

Left: The station house at Hunnington was saved from demolition and is now in residential use, as this view taken in 2001 shows. *Author's collection*

Left: The exterior of the disused Rubery station in February 1966. Prior to World War 1, a walk from the station enabled connections to be made to trams that provided services to the Lickey Hills. Regular passenger services ended in 1919, and the last freight train used the station in 1964. *A. Muckley*

Right: Platform 2 at Longbridge station, looking towards Halesowen. The track ends just beyond this view, but the station was still rail connected to Halesowen Junction to the south when this photograph was taken in February 1966. It is clear that at one time this substantial station, located within the Austin works, would have been well used by workers at the Longbridge car factory. *A. Muckley*

Right: The line to Halesowen runs to the left of this view, under the station buildings at Longbridge, which were used by workmen's trains to New Street until 1960, and were still in use for parcels traffic when this view was taken on 4 June 1966. On the right, *Austin 1*, a Kitson 0-6-0ST dating from 1932, is seen shunting in the works yard with Longbridge-owned wagons. Surprisingly, many of the features seen in this view remained in 2002, including the signalbox and the closed passenger station buildings. *R. Siviter*

Right: Longbridge station, seen here, was located within the car factory until a new station was built on the nearby main line. Although unused and derelict, the station building was still extant when this photograph was taken in September 2001. Plans to reopen this southern part of the branch, as far as Frankley, have been considered. *Author*

15 Desolation at Dudley

With its castle and the long-standing Earls of Dudley, Dudley developed into one of the most important towns in the Black Country. It equally developed as a railway centre. In 1849 the first train arrived in the town on the South Staffordshire Railway from Pleck, near Walsall, but regular goods trains did not start until March of the following year, passenger services commencing in May. The next line to open was the 5¼-mile section of line from Stourbridge to Dudley. This was part of the Oxford, Worcester & Wolverhampton Railway and the section, including the tunnel at Dudley, finally opened to passengers in December 1852. The section northwards to Tipton opened in July the following year and through services were running to Wolverhampton by 1854.

Round Oak was the scene of this country's first major runaway accident, in August 1858. An excursion train returning to Wolverhampton comprising no fewer than 30 coaches, perhaps not too surprisingly, broke a coupling on the 1 in 75 grade near Round Oak. This resulted in 18 coaches running back towards Brettell Lane and hitting the locomotive of a second excursion train, which had already taken on seven coaches from the first train. The accident resulted in 14 dead and 50 badly injured.

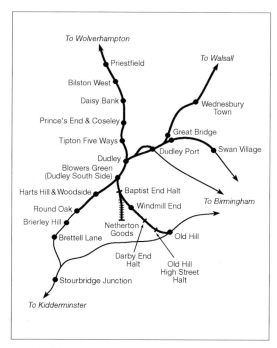

Left: A two-car BRCW DMU waiting empty, south of Dudley station by the massive water tower, to form the 8.18pm to Walsall on 26 August 1961. In 1963, the service was identified in the Beeching Report for closure, and in July 1964 the last train ran, ending all passenger services to Dudley. *M. Mensing*

Above left: By September 1966, when this view was taken, this was the only remaining gas lamp bracket at Dudley station. Soon after, all the buildings were demolished and the former station site was gradually cleared. *A. Dyer*

Above right: The Stephenson Locomotive Society visited Dudley station on 11 September 1966 when this view was taken, following closure to passengers in 1964. At that time the facilities remained largely intact, perhaps almost in a state of shock that such an important settlement in the Black Country could lose its railway station. *A. Dyer*

Right: A map of the Dudley area in 1938. The Black Country Museum is now located on the site marked Guest Hospital. *Crown Copyright*

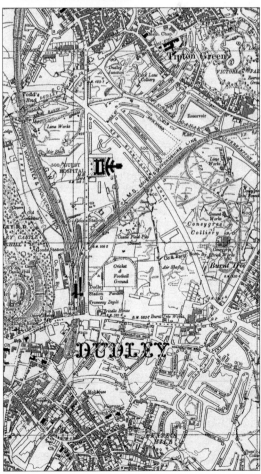

Operating flexibility from Dudley was provided when the South Staffordshire Railway opened a link from the Stour Valley line at Dudley Port in January 1854 and the GWR provided a link from their main line at Swan Village to join the Pleck line in September 1866. The 2¾-mile GWR link to Old Hill was the last line completed to Dudley, opening in March 1878.

Services expanded and as far back as 1872 the LNWR ran through trains from Dudley to Derby. In the 1930s, the LMS had 15 departures to Euston, many with restaurant cars, while the GWR provided 11 trains to Paddington each day. By 1956, there were 11 trains to Euston and 13 to Paddington daily. Routes still ran to Walsall, Wolverhampton, Stourbridge Junction, Birmingham and to Old Hill.

Dudley station, although on one site, was two adjoining stations, one LNWR and the other GWR. The LMS and GWR maintained separate ticket offices and goods sheds and even Nationalisation at first saw Dudley's goods yards provided with two names, Dudley Town LMR and Dudley Castle WR.

In early BR days, Dudley remained a well-served railway town, with extensive facilities and frequent trains, but the situation was to change dramatically. Passenger services to Wolverhampton and Stourbridge were withdrawn in July 1962. The 'Bumble Hole' line to Old Hill closed to passengers in June 1964; the freight link to Netherton closed the following year and the remaining line completely in January 1968. The summer of 1964 saw the last 'Dudley Dodger', the name sometimes given to the shuttle service that ran from Dudley to Dudley Port. The withdrawal of the 'Dasher' services to Walsall and the link via Great Bridge to Snow Hill during the same summer meant that Dudley became the largest town in the area without passenger services. Closure of the route from Stourbridge Junction to Priestfield Junction was generally considered one of the major losses in this part of the country.

After the passenger closures, the former Castle freight yard opened as a Freightliner depot in 1967 and the passenger station at Dudley, together with others on the lines to there, were demolished. In 1972, a new section of line was built at Brettell Lane around an opencast mine, but today there are no remains of the Freightliner yard at Dudley, which finally closed in September 1986. The track through Dudley was mothballed in March 1993 but there are plans for reopening the Stourbridge to Walsall line through the town as a freight route, together with use of sections of

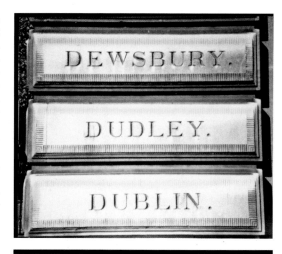

Above: Although the Doric Arch at Euston has been demolished, the side entrance lodges remain and have carved on their quoins an array of 72 destinations once served from the station. Dudley no longer has a direct service to the original station, but the name was still displayed in August 2001. *Author*

this line by the Midland Metro. At Dudley itself the former station site and the Station Hotel, which was rebuilt in 1936, remain in anticipation of passenger trains that may one day serve the town again.

Above: The unusual operating procedure mentioned below continued for many years. Here, a three-car suburban Derby-built DMU is drawing out of the platform at Dudley, to cross over and return to Birmingham Snow Hill, at 4pm on 26 August 1961. The deep cutting in which the station was situated, at the foot of Dudley Hill, is apparent from this view. *M. Mensing*

Left: Well-filled ex-GWR AEC diesel railcar No W13W at Platform 3, Dudley. The GWR began to experiment with diesel traction in the 1930s and constructed a number of distinctive-looking railcars. An unusual operating procedure was involved at Dudley, the unit reversing beyond the signalbox and then reappearing on the other side of the platform as it used the crossover lines on its way to Birmingham Snow Hill. *Ian Allan Library*

Above: Forming the 4.18pm service to Walsall, a two-car DMU waits to leave Dudley station on 26 August 1961. The station was in fact two adjoining stations, the ex-LMS and ex-GWR stations each once having separate booking offices and facilities. The train here is seen on the ex-LMS side of the station. *M. Mensing*

Left: The closed Baptist End Halt on the Dudley-Old Hill 'Bumble Hole' line, looking west in February 1966. New shelters and electric lights were provided, but they were unable to save this line which closed to passengers in June 1964. Local goods facilities were retained at Dudley until August 1966 and this line closed completely in January 1968. *A. Muckley*

Below left: Stanier '8F' 2-8-0 No 48705 brings a banked freight train off the 'Bumble Hole' line. The line was so named because of the number of old flooded pits and canal basins on part of its route. The train is seen here at Old Hill, on a dull June morning in 1966. *A. Muckley*

Above right: The station at Dudley was built in a substantial cutting below the town. When this view was taken, in August 2001, mothballed rusting track ran through the site. In the near foreground, the base of the water tank was still apparent. *Author's collection*

Right: Dudley Tunnel in the summer of 2001, rather more overgrown compared with the view in Chapter 1. The last train to use the tunnel was in 1993, but tracks remain beneath the vegetation. There are proposals for a freight reopening of the line through the station, and Midland Metro use of other sections of the route to Wednesbury. *Author's collection*

16 Withdrawn to Walsall

The Grand Junction's station for Walsall was located to the south of the town near Bescot, but in November 1847, the South Staffordshire Railway provided a link from Bescot to reach a town that was destined to become the focal point of many lines. Indeed Ryecroft Junction, to the north of Walsall, at one time had the distinction of being the only five-way junction on BR.

The South Staffordshire line was extended to Lichfield in April 1849. Another line struck out to Cannock in February 1858, both being destined to become LNWR routes from the Black Country. The Wolverhampton & Walsall Railway opened a 7¼-mile route between the two towns in November 1872; the line was initially bought by the LNWR, but was soon sold to the Midland Railway. The Midland line from Castle Bromwich opened to Walsall in July 1879 and a cut-off line to the north of the town, at Ryecroft, enabled east-west freight trains to avoid Walsall. In March 1881, the LNWR, by means of new curves and

the ex-GJR line, provided a second link from Walsall to Wolverhampton. From 1909 most through passenger trains used this route, as it avoided the need for reversal at Walsall.

Consequently, one of the first major passenger closures in the area was the ex-Midland route to Wolverhampton. Tram competition had assisted in the closure of intermediate stations at Bentley in 1898, Heath Town in 1910 and Walsall North in 1925, but remaining stations closed to passengers in January 1931. The line survived as a through freight route until September 1964, after which a section from Ryecroft Junction to a power station at Birchills endured until May 1980. A western section was also retained to Willenhall Stafford Street until November 1965, when the line was cut back to Wednesfield, which survived as a siding until November 1983. Part of this siding was subsequently converted into a road and much of the line has been identified as a possible future Midland Metro route.

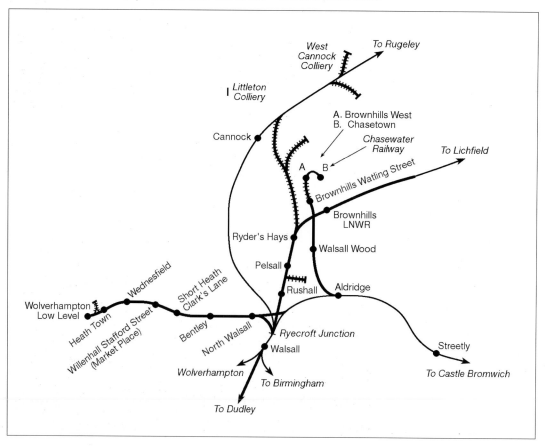

Right: The line near Walsall North, looking south towards Ryecroft Junction in March 2001. Disused railways can represent an ideal opportunity for wildlife to flourish in urban areas. However, on this stretch of line I noticed two urban cats wreaking havoc on the wildlife attempting to live in the disused cutting. (My black cat Nimbus died soon after this view was taken and, like some lost lines, she has gone with sadness, but is not forgotten.) *Author*

Right: Ryecroft Junction in March 2001. An engine shed was once located within the area straight ahead in this view that is now overgrown with mature trees. Before the closure of lines in the area, a further set of double tracks veered off to the right to Brownhills, while another double track veered off to the far left to Wolverhampton, making this the only five-way junction in Britain at one time. *Author*

Right: The 10.20am Birmingham-Leeds train passing Fossway Crossing box on Sunday, 11 February 1973, diverted via Walsall to Ryecroft Junction and thence over the freight-only line to Lichfield City. The warning signal on the up line is for Anglesey Sidings, Brownhills, where Messrs Charringtons had an oil storage depot. The engine is Class 45 No 44. The signalbox and crossing gates were soon to be replaced by automatic half-barriers, but unfortunately, a section of this line was to close in 1984, making its use for passenger diversions no longer an option. *G. Bannister*

Left: The Anglesey Branch Canal passes over the closed line to Lichfield City, to the north of Ryecroft Junction, as this view at Brownhills shows. The original railway builders would be surprised to find the use of the canal continues, while the railway closed in January 1984. A single track remains in the undergrowth from Lichfield to a point just south of the iron canal bridge in this view, taken in August 2001. *Author*

While the MR route to Wolverhampton was a significant early passenger closure, at the same time an extensive range of services had developed from Walsall to Dudley, Lichfield, Wolverhampton, Rugeley and Birmingham with some through trains to London. The lines and services survived World War 2, while after the war, modernisation took place, including the electrification of services to Birmingham, and all looked well.

A great upheaval came in the wake of the Beeching Report. This seemed to declare war on Walsall and identified every single passenger service from the town for closure. There were even plans for the Walsall electric services to Birmingham to be replaced with buses. There was an outcry and the electric services to Birmingham were reprieved, but all other lines were to close to passengers. The first to go were the services to Dudley Port and Dudley in July 1964, while passenger services from Walsall to Wolverhampton, Lichfield, Castle Bromwich and Rugeley all closed in January 1965.

Fortunately, freight services continued on some of the lines, although the northern cut-off line at Ryecroft closed in 1967, while the line to Anglesey Sidings closed in March 1984, which taken together with other closures, reduced Ryecroft to a two-way junction. However, a turning point was beginning to appear. The freight-only line from Walsall to Hednesford reopened to passengers in April 1989 and was extended to Rugeley in June 1997. The ex-LNWR line to Wolverhampton was reopened to passengers in May 1998 and the line to Dudley has been mothballed with plans for reopening for freight. Today, Walsall has a busy and thriving new station, showing the complete folly of the Beeching proposals for the town.

Left: Timetable, Walsall-Dudley, April 1910

Below: Timetable, Walsall-Dudley, July 1955.

WALSALL, WEDNESBURY, and DUDLEY.—London and North Western.

(Timetable, April 1910 — Up and Down, Week Days and Sundays)

D Runs via Princes End.   S Saturdays only.

Table 84 — WALSALL, WEDNESBURY and DUDLEY

(Timetable, July 1955 — Week Days only)

E Except Saturdays
S Saturdays only
For LOCAL TRAINS between Dudley Port and Dudley, see Table 85.

Right: A view from the footplate of the 1.20pm Saturdays-only goods train leaving Walsall with ex-LNWR 0-8-0 No 49371, running tender first, on 20 May 1950. *P. B. Whitehouse*

Below: Ex-LNWR 0-8-0s Nos 48895 and 49430 make a brief stop at Walsall to attach wagons to the 9.30am Water Orton-Willenhall (Stafford Street) train on 18 October 1964. Four such locomotives were retained at Bescot for this service, but were withdrawn later that year. *R. Shenton*

Above: Two three-car Birmingham-built Metro-Cammell DMUs on the Stephenson Locomotive Society's '50th Anniversary Birmingham Railtour' special, heading eastwards along the ex-MR Walsall avoiding line and crossing the Walsall-Rugeley line at Ryecroft on 30 May 1959. This avoiding section of line closed in 1967 and this particular part is now a footpath, with a new footbridge crossing over the Rugeley line at this point. *M. Mensing*

Left: A section of the ex-LNWR Brownhills-Ryecroft Junction line is now used as a footpath, which does not help the prospect of trains running through to Lichfield again. Here, a signal post survives on the route near Brownhills in August 2001. *Author's collection*

Below: A cast-iron road sign to the closed Pelsall station could still be seen in August 2001. All trace of the station, which closed in 1965, has long since gone. However, Pelsall survived its adjoining stations by many years. An intermediate station to the north, called Ryder's Hays, closed in 1858 and one to the south, called Rushall, closed in March 1909. *Author*

Below: The Southern Electric Group's 'Walsall Concerto' railtour, hauled by a Class 50, passes Dudley Port on the freight-only Walsall-Stourbridge line on 27 June 1987. The line was subsequently closed, but was mothballed for future freight or Midland Metro use. *C. Morrison*

Right: The Walsall-Stourbridge line was abandoned after the last train ran in March 1993 and a section is seen here near Dudley Port, currently unused when this view was taken in August 2000, but saved from complete demolition. *Author*

Inset: Timetable for September 1964, announcing closure of the Walsall-Dudley service.

WALSALL AND DUDLEY

The service on this table is withdrawn and Wednesbury Town, Great Bridge North, Dudley Port Low Level and Dudley stations are closed. The locality is served by Omnibuses operated by Walsall Corporation Transport, the Birmingham and Midland Motor Omnibus Co. Ltd., West Bromwich Corporation Transport and Birmingham City Transport.

17 Coal from Cannock

The hills of south Staffordshire form part of Cannock Chase and this area remained rural until coal was found under Cannock, and from 1770 an ever-increasing number of collieries developed to feed Black Country industries. The collieries became rail connected and at one time a network of lines resulted in an extensive number of coal trains running from the area into the Black Country and Birmingham.

There was considerable rivalry to serve the area. The South Staffordshire Railway opened lines to Cannock and Norton from Walsall in February 1858 and these were soon extended and taken over by the LNWR. The MR Walsall Wood branch from Aldridge opened to freight traffic in April 1882 and was extended to Norton in November the same year. A passenger service was introduced on the four-mile section between Aldridge and Brownhills in 1884. The Midland station at Brownhills was inconveniently sited to the northwest of the town and the line was little used by passengers, particularly as an alternative LNWR direct service to Walsall existed. The MR branch was closed to passengers in March 1930, but coal freight continued until collieries in the Chasewater area closed in 1960. Much of the remaining line survived until

Left: Ex-LNWR 0-8-0 No 49371, having come off a coal train, is seen at the once busy Norton Junction on 29 May 1950. All has now been closed. *P. B. Whitehouse*

Left: Brownhills, with the ex-MR route leading to collieries in the Cannock area in 1947. Passenger services were withdrawn in 1930, but coal trains continued to use the ever-diminishing sections of the line for another 35 years. *Ian Allan Library*

1962, after which further cut-backs saw the last short siding link at Aldridge close in 1969.

The extensive and complex network of colliery railways which served coal pits in the Cannock area gradually withered away. The line from West Cannock Colliery to the main line near Hednesford was one of the last to survive. Nevertheless, the line from Littleton Colliery to reception sidings near Penkridge was the last colliery railway to close in the area and this was the last pit to close, in 1993. The spoil tips from the former collieries have mostly disappeared and the swathes of attractive heathland in this area encourage tourism.

The Chasewater Railway at Brownhills operates as the 'Colliery Line', reflecting its origins and location in the centre of the Cannock coalfield. The line was once an integral part of the coal industry in this area, but is now an important element of the tourist industry. The Birmingham Northern Relief Road cut through part of the original preserved railway in recent years, and as a result, the original terminus of the preserved line at Chasewater was closed and the line extended with new stations constructed.

Above: West Cannock Colliery in Staffordshire, with Bagnall 0-6-0ST *Topham* heading a train of empties on 24 October 1969. A mineral line from the north of Hednesford station directly served the colliery. Note the enclosed footbridge. *R. Siviter*

Below: The Littleton Colliery railway on 5 September 1969, as *Littleton No 5*, a Manning, Wardle 0-6-0ST built in 1922, with empties nears the colliery. At one time eight steam locomotives were available for work on the 3½-mile colliery railway. Little remains of the colliery, but some traces of the railway, which linked the pit to the reception sidings on the main line, can still be found. *R. Siviter*

Below: On the Littleton Colliery line, *Littleton No 7*, a Hudswell, Clarke-built 0-6-0ST, crosses Cannock Chase with empties for the colliery on 4 May 1970. At this time, work on upgrading and repairing the track was still being undertaken. *R. Siviter*

Above: Littleton No 5 crosses the Staffordshire & Worcestershire Canal with a permanent way train. Note the size of the locomotive's cab. Coal from Littleton Colliery was used at power stations in the area. Despite impressive productivity improvements, the colliery finally closed in 1993 and the railway was subsequently lifted. Plans to turn the pit head buildings into a museum did not come to fruition, and little remains today. R. Siviter

Left: Robert Nelson No 4, a Hunslet 0-6-0ST, shunts at Littleton Colliery yard assisted by a Yorkshire diesel on 5 September 1969. Littleton Colliery was the last traditional rail-connected pit to survive in the area. A fleet of steam locomotives (some of which survive in preservation) continued to operate the mineral railway until 1978, when diesels took over the remaining workings. R. Siviter

Below: The Colliery Line, as the Chasewater Railway is known, has preserved sections of colliery railways in the area. Here, No 11 Alfred Paget, a Neilson 0-4-0ST dating from 1882, hauls a freight train, including a Cannock Chase coal wagon, near the Chasewater Reservoir on 12 October 1980, evoking the sights and sounds of the past. A small section of the preserved line has itself been closed to make way for the Birmingham Northern Relief Road, but the line has also been considerably extended subsequently. A. Pearson

18 Lost and Lingering Legacies

The area had its fair share of attractive railway buildings, but the nature of its industries was functional and many buildings were also functional in their design. Some of the finest railway buildings were among the earliest, as the railway arrived on the grand scale. Hardwick's original L&B terminus at Birmingham Curzon Street was arguably the greatest of all the railway buildings in the area with its huge stone Ionic columns and façade, to mirror the Euston Arch at the other end of the line, and indeed the building nearly ended up with the same fate. Once its office use ended by 1968, BR had no love of the building, but fortunately the citizens of Birmingham recognised their treasure and the main part of the massively imposing building remains.

Although many railway buildings were built to last, few have survived. Almost everything of the original Birmingham New Street station and the railway-owned

Above: The one surviving original gateway to Snow Hill station, now bricked up in Livery Street. The fine brown terracotta tiles and GWR crest give a hint of the ornateness of the original station. This view was taken in the summer of 2000. *Author*

Above right: A great monument to the Industrial Revolution. The main building at Curzon Street opened in 1838 and was the first L&B station in Birmingham. The station boasted a number of other firsts. It provided the first railway hotel in the world and the first ever railway refreshment room, for passengers only. The first female clerks were also employed on the site in 1874, after it had been converted to a goods yard. After a long spell as a goods office the enormous and elegant building, with its four massive Ionic columns and crest of the L&B, was listed and preserved. The entrance is seen here in the summer of 2001. *Author*

Right: A fake, the Midland Hotel at Birmingham had nothing to do with the Midland Railway, but was so named to attract customers from the LNWR's Queens Hotel opposite. Although long since renamed, the 'Midland Hotel' still appears prominently on the current hotel's walls. The hotel remains open, as this view taken in August 2001 shows. *Author*

hotel have been demolished. William Livock designed New Street station's adjoining hotel, known as the Queens Hotel. It was opened in 1854, replacing a smaller hotel at Curzon Street. The graceful and symmetrical white brick hotel at New Street was extended in 1911, 1917 and 1925 to eventually provide over 200 rooms. Queen Victoria, King George V, General de Gaulle, Khrushchev and Mae West were amongst its many guests. The hotel was closed and demolished, amidst protests, in 1966. Some chandeliers were transferred to the Adelphi Hotel in Liverpool and by way of small consolation, an Ian Allan bookshop is to be found on the site today.

The Midland Hotel was built opposite to New Street station. Its name implied that it was a railway hotel, although it was not owned by the Midland Railway and it was simply named as such as a marketing ploy. The hotel still remains, although it has been renamed.

The Great Western Hotel, at Birmingham Snow Hill station, was opened in 1863 and purchased by the GWR in 1906. It sustained damage during World War 2 and was closed and converted to offices, although the ground floor refreshment facilities remained in use until its demolition in 1970. Snow Hill, with its embellishments, was despised in the 1960s, but would now have been revered for its reassuring solid

Right: The Queen's Building at Wolverhampton in July 2000. The handsome and symmetrical Italianate-looking building dates from 1849 and was designed by Edward Banks. It provided access to the LNWR Queen Street station, later known as the High Level station, some distance away on the other side of a canal. Later it was used as a goods office, but after a period of dereliction, the Queen's Building currently provides a café for use in association with the adjoining bus station. *Author*

Right: The listed classical façade of Wolverhampton Low Level station in July 2000. The imposing blue brick and stone dressings of the station buildings were designed by John Fowler, but the buildings are currently unused and possibly at risk unless a new use is forthcoming. *Author*

ornateness. Only a gateway and a few ruins of the original station remain.

At Wolverhampton, another most unusual white brick and sandstone building has been saved. The Italianate opulence of the original Shrewsbury & Birmingham Railway station coach entrance, dating from 1849 known as Queen's Building, and designed by Edward Banks, was some way from the station platforms and has survived. Queen Street station, renamed High Level from 1885 to 1972, with its overall roof, was demolished and renewed. However, the unique GWR Wolverhampton Low Level station, with its blue engineering bricks and classical façade, designed by John Fowler, remains. The current station was remodelled from the original 1855 building in 1869, but in 2002, since its final closure in 1981, it has been in a mainly unused and vulnerable condition.

The station buildings at Dudley have gone completely and the huge station site cleared, although the imposing privately run Station Hotel, situated above the old station cutting, remains and retains its name in anticipation of trains that will surely one day return. At Walsall, the original station has been largely subsumed in a shopping precinct. Elsewhere when stations were closed there seemed to be a race by BR to demolish them, so few disused stations remain. The Midland Railway stations were particularly distinctive, but only a small number of original buildings are extant today.

The race to demolish goods buildings by BR was equally ferocious, although some of the buildings once associated with railway freight still remain in the area. In particular, ex-LNWR goods sheds at Wednesbury, Walsall and Wolverhampton all survived into 2002.

Left: On an altogether smaller scale was the original Hampton station, built by the Birmingham & Derby Junction Railway and dating from 1839. This view was taken in July 2001 before the surrounding vegetation was removed, allowing the building once again to be seen from the main ex-L&B railway. Replaced by a new station at Hampton in 1884, this was attractively renamed Hampton-in-Arden from 1886. *Author*

Centre left: King's Norton station was remodelled in 1926 by the LMS. The earlier buildings, which were typical of many MR stations in the area, were long disused when this view was taken in August 2001. *Author*

Left: Part of the outer walling of the ex-LNWR goods depot at Windsor Street survives, much of the former railway yard now being in industrial use. Most buildings associated with the depot have been demolished, but a symmetrical red-brick building, once used as the canteen on the site of the depot has survived, as seen in this view taken in August 2001. *Author*

19 Private Sidings and Railways

There were once large numbers of private sidings linking into the main railway network around Birmingham and the Black Country. They provided lifeblood to the system and served mineral workings, depots and works of every variety. All the industrial landmarks in the area, such as the steel works at Round Oak, Bilston and Wednesbury, the coal-fired power stations at Tipton, Birchills, Hams Hall and Nechells, and the numerous main gas works, were all once served by rail systems. By the mid-1980s all had closed.

The diversity of the private lines and sidings was apparent from just a few examples. In Birmingham alone, a list of over 125 sidings still in operation after World War 2 reads like a 'who's who' list of trades for the city itself. BSA at Small Heath, Chad Valley at Harborne, the CWS at Bromford Bridge, Birmingham Corporation's Public Works Department at Soho Pool, the Patent Enamel Co at Selly Oak and United Glass Bottle Manufacturers at Crawford are just a small selection of the private and municipal concerns that once had sidings connected to the main railway

Right: A typical Peckett 0-4-0ST, seen here in March 1966, shunting at Bromford Bridge, Birmingham Corporation's lamp-post and stores depot. This was one of several rail-connected depots operated by the city council. *A. Muckley*

Right: Seen here on the internal network at Hams Hall Power Station in March 1966 is 0-6-0T No 10, built by Robert Stephenson & Hawthorns. The faded words on the tank sides are 'Central Electricity Authority No. 10 Midlands Division'. *A. Muckley*

network. A number of sidings were of considerable length and some developed into private railways.

Of the private railways, the Pensnett Railway was the most extensive. A complex network of mineral lines developed from the Shutt End Railway after 1846 and, following many additions, at one time over 40 miles of track were in use and the railway employed over 150 staff. An annual passenger service was provided on the Baggeridge Colliery line for the Himley fêtes between 1929 and 1937. The 1950s saw closures, while diesel operation had replaced most steam workings by 1963. In 1968, Baggeridge Colliery ceased production and the main Round Oak steel works to Baggeridge Junction section of railway also closed. The last remains were to be found at Round Oak steel works until this ceased operating in December 1982. All is now closed, although as mentioned previously, an ex-GWR link from Kingswinford Junction to Pensnett remains in situ.

Above: Rubery Owen & Co at Darlaston operated *Mars*, an 0-4-0ST Peckett built in 1915 and seen here in August 1963. The firm produced metal products and closed in 1980. The engine and associated sidings were typical of many private railways in the area. *P. Hocquard*

Left: A goods shed and facilities for handling 225 wagons were built at Curzon Street specifically to handle the valuable ICI metals traffic. At the ICI Metals Division itself, this Hibberd 'Planet' four-wheel diesel locomotive, named *Stour*, is seen at the Kynoch Works at Witton near Birmingham. *L. J. Shepherd*

Left: Sam was purchased from BR (Class 02 No D2868) and is seen at the LCP coal concentration depot at Pensnett near Dudley on 10 August 1978. The once extensive network of mineral railways and sidings in this area is now closed, together with the Pensnett Railway. The BR Kingswinford Junction-Pensnett line remains, but the depot and line are currently out of use. *D. Habgood*

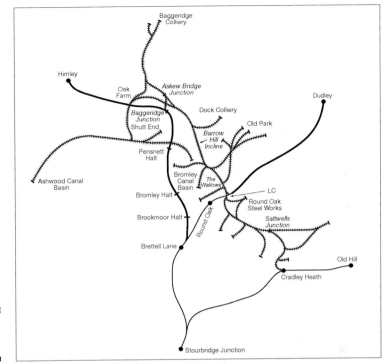

The railway system at the Fort Dunlop rubber plant, at Bromford Bridge near Birmingham, served the Dunlop factory until steam use ended by 1970. The 0-4-0ST locomotives used on the line included an ex-MoD Bagnall and two former CWS Irlam Pecketts. All were preserved after the system was replaced by rubber-wheeled road traffic.

At Stirchley Street, Bournville was added to the name in 1880 to reflect the nearby chocolate factory. In 1879, Cadbury ran a fleet of narrowboats and only ceased use of the canals in 1961. The Cadbury Railway, serving the factory at Bournville, also connected with the nearby Worcester & Birmingham Canal. Opened in 1884, at one time the railway had almost 5 miles of track, although it was always known as 'the siding'. Coke was used to fire the steam engines to reduce pollution at the factory and in 1957 the first diesel locomotive arrived. Cocoa, sugar and coal arriving by rail and the dispatch of completed products to Cadbury depots (see *Lost Lines: London*) was gradually transferred to road and the line closed in May 1976. One of the steam locomotives used on the system is preserved at Tyseley.

Herbert Austin selected the factory at Longbridge as a greenfield site because the paint on his cars would dry better than in the smog of Birmingham. The site gave birth to the Austin Seven and provided armaments that helped win two world wars. The works has an internal railway system that opened in 1915 and developed to serve a more extensive factory complex, including a foundry, but in 2002 sidings still ran into the MG Rover works.

Above: The Fort Dunlop works with a Peckett-built 0-4-0ST shunting on 20 May 1969. This and two other two Dunlop engines were saved from scrap after steam operations ended by 1970. Although no longer rail served, the famous Dunlop factory remains in use on this site. *R. Siviter*

Below: The Cadbury line with *Avonside* 0-4-0T No 4 on the works 'siding' which opened in 1884. The engine dated from 1910 and was the first of the Avonsides to be taken out of service, being scrapped in 1954. At its peak, up to six locomotives could be found in operation, but the system closed completely in May 1976. *Ian Allan Library*

Right: Cadbury sidings.

Upper right: Cadbury Bournville locomotive No 1, an Avonside 0-4-0T dating from 1925, was preserved by the Dowty Railway Preservation Society, but was subsequently moved to the Birmingham Railway Museum at Tyseley. It is seen here being greeted by Sir Adrian Cadbury (right) and Michael Whitehouse, then Chairman of the trustees of the Birmingham Railway Museum, on its return to Birmingham in November 1988. Four of Cadbury's covered goods vans found their way to the Severn Valley Railway.
Ian Allan Library

Centre right: The most substantial engineering structure on the Cadbury line was a bridge that carried the railway from the chocolate factory over the Midland main line and the Worcester & Birmingham Canal to a canal wharf. The bridge still exists to this day, as this view taken in August 2001 shows. The famous chocolate factory also remains in production.
Author

Lower right: Austin 1, a Kitson 0-6-0ST built in 1932, shunts at the Longbridge works on 4 June 1966. The engine was once part of a fleet of nine engines. British Leyland purchased the sidings within the works from BR in 1968. Some older parts of the factory and associated rail networks have subsequently been removed. *R. Siviter*

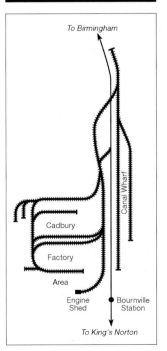

To Birmingham

Canal Wharf

Cadbury

Factory

Area

Engine
Shed

Bournville
Station

To King's Norton

Above: The Longbridge car factory once had its own power station and foundry, and all were rail connected. Here, *Austin 3*, a Hunslet 0-6-0ST built in 1937, shunts coal wagons at Longbridge in November 1968. The MG Rover works remains rail connected and a reduced network of lines still allows for the despatch of cars by rail. *A. Muckley*

Left: A close-up of the massive *Vulcan*, a Bagnall 0-6-0ST dating from 1950 at Longbridge in November 1968. It was used at the works until diesels gradually replaced steam traction in the 1960s. The engine has since been preserved. *A. Muckley*

20 Maglev and Monorail

This area has always been associated with innovation and invention. Thus it was that at one time, two most unusual private railways were in operation. The first unique line was the Maglev link which connected the main line to Birmingham Airport. Maglev, which is short for magnetic levitation, was not strictly a railway because a linear induction motor powered the passenger cars, which in effect floated over the 'track' without wheels or a driver. The route ran from a high level station at Birmingham International on an elevated concrete viaduct to the airport. Opened successfully in 1985, the link was included in railway timetables as operating at 'frequent intervals' and with a journey time of two minutes. The system closed as life-expired in June 1995, ending the only commercial passenger Maglev system in the country, although one of the Maglev cars has gone to Railworld, Peterborough.

The second unique line to open was a monorail. Passenger monorails date back to the 1870s, but their use has been limited. One of the very few to be provided in the UK once served the Merry Hill shopping centre near Dudley. Merry Hill was itself built on the site of the former Round Oak steel works that closed in 1982. The development and its monorail

Above & right: The Maglev track is seen here winding its way from Birmingham International station to Birmingham Airport. It shows the central flat section that was used as a reaction rail for the linear motor in each Maglev car. A pair of cars ran the service, each having a capacity of 32 passengers. They were suspended 15mm above the track by magnetism and propelled by waves of electric current. In these views engineers fiddle with the automatic link on 21 July 1984, but it did not come into full use until the middle of the following year.
Ian Allan Library/ John Glover

could not have been more different from the former works.

The monorail was built over the rooftops of the shopping centre and four stations were included on its curving and graded route. Opened in June 1991, a two-way shuttle system ran on an elevated almost square steel box girder with a top plate providing the running surface. The monorail was supported on steel columns with a minimum height in areas with traffic of 20ft. It was provided with a 500V ac conductor rail mounted below the running surface, to provide traction to the rolling stock.

The monorail included a traversing track section, repeating history from the traverser at Moor Street. An extension of the line to Waterfront West station, which would have been close to the A461 road, was never constructed and the remaining 2¼-mile system fell into disuse in 1995 due to technical problems. By the summer of 2001, Central station, located above Marks & Spencer and the lift to its covered platforms were the last remains, but elsewhere the infrastructure had been dismantled and, together with the trains, dispatched to a monorail at Broadbeach in Australia.

Both these systems were at the forefront of innovation and are two of the most unusual lost lines covered in this series. However, the Maglev route has been reconstituted as a fully automated Cable Liner Shuttle, while the Midland Metro, Line 3, will provide a new tram route to Merry Hill.

Right: Merry Hill monorail.

Below: The UK's first urban transport monorail system operated at the Merry Hill shopping centre at Brierley Hill. The Swiss-built aluminium rolling stock was capable of speeds of up to 20mph, and four seven-car units could each carry over 100 passengers. One of the trains is seen here leaving Central station, on the extreme left, which was connected to the shopping centre by a lift. *Ian Allan Library*

21 Goods Gone By

Industry boomed in Victorian times and the railways at one time carried a huge amount of the area's freight. Such were the volumes of traffic that freight trains were obliged to run throughout the night. By way of example, each night, even in the 1950s, 15 long-distance freight trains departed or arrived at Wolverhampton. There were local freight facilities and major depots, many of which required expansion to cope with the ever-increasing volumes of traffic. The freight facilities were almost as varied as the goods traffic the trains once carried.

After World War 2 there was a complete transformation and almost all forms of rail freight witnessed significant decreases in traffic. The decline was particularly rapid on individual wagon loads and BR began to actively discourage small amounts of rail freight. Rationalisation to deal with the contraction saw many closures, as remaining rail freight was

Right: Stanier Class 3 2-6-2T No 40118 is seen here shunting two vans at the end of Platform 6, Birmingham New Street station, on 12 June 1958. Originally intended as a loading dock for horses, when this view was taken perishable, parcels and small goods were handled as an integral part of the old passenger station's freight sidings. *M. Mensing*

Right: Diesel-electric shunter No D3840 shunts wagons into sidings at the end of Platform 6 at New Street on 18 February 1961. Passengers are clearly visible and on occasions the goods vans contained fish, so you can begin to understand the complaints about unpleasant odours at the old station! *M. Mensing*

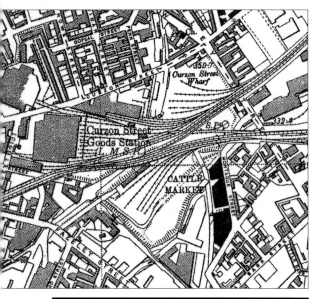

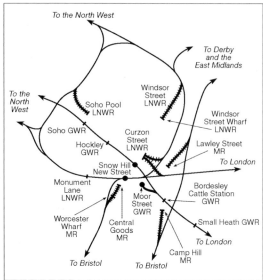

concentrated at an ever-decreasing number of locations. In an act of rationalisation in the area, BR concentrated the work of 168 coal yards into just five depots. Consequently, it can be seen that the following examples provide just a glimpse of the vast range of freight facilities that once operated in the area.

The need to increase passenger facilities at Birmingham led to some of the early smaller passenger stations becoming obsolete and the opportunity to use these sites as goods depots was seized upon. At Curzon Street, the original L&B station building became a splendid goods office, when the adjoining area was converted for use as a freight depot. At its peak the depot had a capacity of over 1,000 wagons, employed 2,000 people and used over 600 working horses. The depot closed by 1966 and the buildings were subsequently demolished, as were those of the adjacent Grand Junction station, which had also been converted to freight use. Fortunately part of the original L&B station building was saved.

The original passenger station at Camp Hill was opened in 1840, but became a goods depot for the Midland Railway when the line was extended to Saltley in 1864. The depot and the line to it survived until February 1966.

Suffolk Street was the MR's central goods depot at Birmingham and opened in 1887. Access to the depot

Left: Canal freight once interchanged with the railway. Here, Class 5700 0-6-0PT No 4696 shunts at Halesowen Canal Basin on 22 September 1966. The railway provided an important link to the Dudley Canal at this point, but canal freight was in terminal decline at this time and disused metal canal barges can be seen in the foreground. *J. Hunt*

Right: Class 5700 0-6-0PT No 8767 works a local coal train at Handsworth & Smethwick station during March 1966. The local, loose-coupled freight train had been a feature of the area since the railways were first opened, but when this view was taken it was about to come to an end. In general, coal and metal freight were important in the area. *A. Muckley*

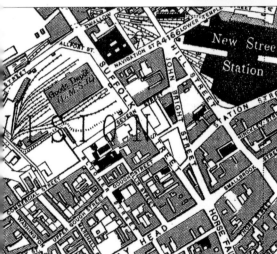

Below: A map of the Midland's central Birmingham goods depot in Suffolk Street in 1938. The closeness of the depot to New Street station is apparent. *Crown Copyright*

involved extending the original passenger line by tunnelling under and diverting the Worcester & Birmingham Canal. A new lower level passenger line also tunnelled through to New Street, while a high level line ran to the canal itself. The depot and associated freight lines closed in March 1967. Much of the Suffolk Street site became railway offices called Stanier House.

On the northern side of the city centre a specially constructed LNWR freight branch from Aston, almost one mile long, reached the Windsor Street goods depot. The depot opened in 1880 to serve central Birmingham. It was extended in 1901 and the 12-acre site could then handle about 800 wagons. The branch was electrified in 1966, but closed in May 1980. Some buildings and walls still remain.

The Soho Pool branch was opened for freight by the LNWR in April 1889 and had the capacity to handle about 500 wagons. It closed in May 1974, although the

Right: An ex-MR Johnson 0-6-0 on a special train at Birmingham Central goods depot in the 1950s. Several enthusiast specials were run to the freight yards in the area before they closed. *D. Lawrence*

Left: Class 46 No 46055 at the head of the 10.25 Taunton-Manchester service, on its approach to Birmingham New Street on 6 September 1977. The trackbed on the left once led to Suffolk Street, the ex-MR central Birmingham goods depot. The trackbed to the depot and to the Worcester Canal remain, but Suffolk Street depot has been used in part for railway offices, appropriately named Stanier House. *Les Bertram*

Left: At one time, working horses undertook a considerable amount of shunting operations and the forward carriage of goods from the depots. The remains of extensive stables were still to be found at the Windsor Street goods depot when this view was taken in August 2000. BR last used horses for shunting in 1964. *Author*

Left: The area was noted as the home of many inventions. The BSA Truck Mover, seen in this view, was designed to operate in railway marshalling yards and sidings and to take the place of horses, winches and shunting engines. One operator could handle the motor mower-like machine. The first ever Truck Mover was put into use at the ex-GWR Hockley goods depot, where this view of it being demonstrated was taken on 6 April 1949. *Ian Allan Library*

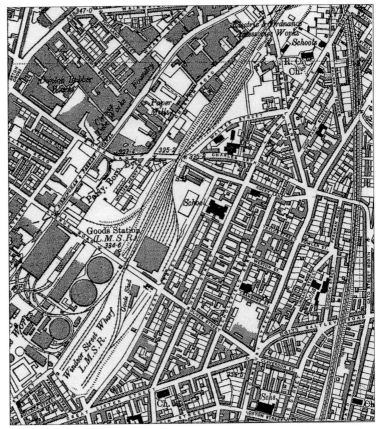

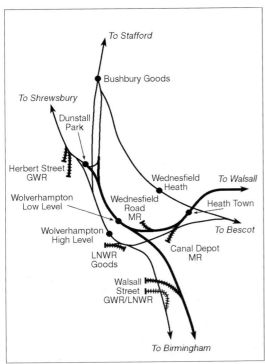

branch remained open to an oil terminal until 1982. Today, little remains of the depot or the route to it.

The GWR had a number of substantial freight facilities in the Birmingham area. Small Heath had a capacity for 1,336 wagons. Bordesley sidings were not too far behind, with a capacity for 1,291 wagons. Hockley goods depot, just outside Snow Hill, had links to the canal network until 1958 and two huge covered sheds for in and out goods. The yard was linked by a dedicated freight line along the main line to a second yard at Soho & Winson Green. Hockley and associated facilities closed in 1971. The goods depot at Moor Street opened in 1914 and had a capacity for 200 wagons. In addition to a large shed to the west of the station, a depot and stables were provided in Park Street below. Two wagon hoists were used to link the two levels. The goods facilities at Moor Street were one of the last to close, in November 1972, and all other remaining ex-GWR general freight facilities in the Birmingham area closed soon after.

In the Wolverhampton area Oxley yards developed as a major interchange for the GWR. By the time the railways were nationalised the yards were massive, capable of holding almost 2,000 wagons, but as the number of wagon loads decreased, the use of the yards declined. The final yard closed in 1969. Another GWR facility at Wolverhampton of particular interest was a

Above: Ivatt Class 2 2-6-0 No 46457 shunts wagons at Birmingham Moor Street station in June 1966. The upper freight shed, which was over 400ft long, to the rear of this view, was still in use at this time. It was demolished after closure of the freight depot in 1972 and the area used as a car park. Subsequently, a new road was cut into the viaduct on which the former goods shed stood as part of the Bull Ring development. *A. Muckley*

Below: The variety of goods facilities in the area was enormous. This picture shows the former Bordesley General and Metal Warehouse, a strongly built concrete structure which was of particularly utilitarian design. The view here was taken on 10 April 1975 and Class 46 No 46049 is about to join the ex-GWR main line with a train of rails. *Philip Hawkins*

Below: A map of part of Bushbury exchange sidings in 1928. *Crown Copyright*

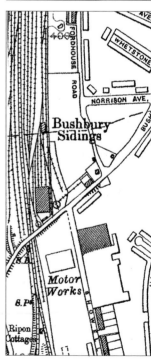

Above: Ex-LNWR 0-8-0 No 49407 heads out of Bushbury Sidings with a heavy freight train for Bescot on 13 July 1964. Note the erection of electrification gantries. The former exchange sidings were closed and the area redeveloped. *P. J. Russell*

Right: The GWR used the 1929 Loans Guarantees Act to demolish the old depot at Victoria Basin at Wolverhampton and build the new Herbert Street goods depot. The huge new depot opened in 1930 and was completed the following year. In 1960 over 180 were still employed on the site and 120 railway lorries also operated from the depot. The depot closed in 1972, but the main goods shed is still extant, albeit in much altered form, and the entrance weighbridge also survives, seen here in January 2002. *Author*

mile-long freight branch that ran from Dunstall Park to serve Herbert Street depot. The depot started life in 1858, as a transhipment facility between broad and standard gauge lines. This lasted until 1869, when it was developed as an ordinary goods depot and the line to serve it was converted to standard gauge. In 1930, the depot was rebuilt and extended, but from 1967 it was used only by National Carriers. The depot closed in March 1972, although tracks remained in situ until 1982.

Elsewhere in Wolverhampton a LNWR goods depot was located close to the High Level station, while the main MR depot was in Wednesfield Road. By the early 1990s both depots were disused and in 1996 the substantial ex-Midland buildings were demolished, but the ex-LNWR buildings still remain. A similar

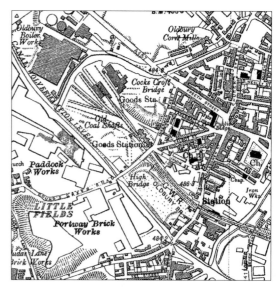

situation exists at Walsall, with some ex-LNWR goods buildings outlasting those of the MR.

At Oldbury the ¾-mile GWR branch from Langley Green to the town had closed to passengers in 1915, but freight lasted much longer and there were extensive facilities here until 1964. Indeed, a short section of the line at Langley Green remained in use to a chemical plant until 1994, when closure came mainly as a result of the chemical trains not being able to use the Channel Tunnel. The track on this section remained in situ in 2001, but all trace of the railway at Oldbury has disappeared under redevelopment.

The yard at Stourbridge was closed in 1965, with the loss of 200 jobs. At Stourbridge Town, a line ran down from the passenger station to the Stourbridge

Left: A view inside the received traffic portion of the sundries shed at Walsall depot, looking from the country end, showing sorting and loading into road vehicles. After offloading from rail wagons and marking with destinations, consignments were loaded on to conveyors and into road vehicles. During the course of writing this book, the remaining railway parcels services, branded as Red Star, ceased to operate. BR

canal basin. The basin closed in July 1965 and Stourbridge Town freight depot in September of the same year. Nearby freight branches to Hayes Lane closed in August 1964 and to Corngreaves Colliery in April 1965.

Newer facilities were not immune from closure. Dudley Freightliner depot began operations in November 1967, on the site of the Castle goods yard. At one time, trains ran direct to Nottingham and Glasgow, while the Newcastle-Cardiff Freightliner also called at Dudley. The new depot looked set for a long-term future, but it was not to be. It was officially closed in September 1986, but much traffic had been transferred to Lawley Street at Birmingham prior to

this date. The site at Dudley was subsequently cleared of all facilities.

In conclusion, there has been a continuous decline in general rail freight in the area. During the course of writing this book the Red Star rail parcel services ended and it was announced that the Travelling Post Offices, which originated from Birmingham in 1838, were to be withdrawn. Nevertheless, rail freight is far from dead and both heavy and new rail freight flows continue to develop in the area.

Right: In Railfreight livery, Class 20 No 20108 arrives at Langley Green from Bescot with chlorine tanks for the Albright & Wilson chemical works. (Albright was the inventor of the safety match.) At this time, freight still used the remaining spur of the ex-GWR Oldbury branch, which can just be seen to the left of this view taken on 11 August 1987. *C. Morrison*

Right: Rails awaiting a reawakening? The branch platform for Oldbury and the track on this part of the branch still remained at Langley Green in August 2001. Ironically, the remaining freight service ended when the chlorine tank wagons operating over the branch were prevented from using the newly opened Channel Tunnel. *Author's collection*

Below: Dudley Freightliner depot with Class 45 No 45029 passing on a Bescot-St Blazey train of china clay empties on 16 May 1985. The terminal and new signalbox opened in 1967 on the site of the Castle goods yard and was the first Freightliner depot in the area. Services were transferred to Birmingham Lawley Street and the Dudley depot finally closed in 1986. The site was subsequently cleared of all equipment, while the signalbox suffered an arson attack in 1988. The last freight trains used the remaining tracks here in 1993. *R. Pynde*

There are many closed passenger stations in the area, on lines that remain open either for freight or for all traffic. Individual station losses date back to the early days of railways, when rationalisation and expansion saw some closures. World War 1 stretched the resources of the railways and forced them to look carefully at their services, and a trickle of closures came forward at that time. In a few cases, stations were closed for operational or rationalisation reasons, while in other examples, changes in the population or industry of the area played a part in the demise of the local station. The tram, bus and car ensured that closures continued right up to the 1970s, but they peaked as a deliberate policy in the 'Beeching years' of

Left: Pleck station opened in 1881, closed as a World War 1 economy measure, but reopened in May 1924. This view is looking north with a DMU approaching. The single passenger did not augur well and the station finally closed in November 1958. *W. A. Camwell*

Left: The disused passenger station at Lifford. This was in fact the third station to serve the town, opening in 1885 when a new junction was built there. Passenger services were withdrawn in 1941, as a wartime economy measure. The station was never to reopen, as closure to passengers was confirmed in 1946. The disused sidings seen here led to a coal yard when this view was taken in January 1969. *A. Muckley*

Right: Winson Green station was added to the busy Stour Valley line in 1876 and was close to the prison of the same name. The station is seen here with 'Jubilee' class No 45647 *Sturdee* passing in August 1957. The neatly kept station closed the following month, together with some other intermediate stations on this line. *Ian Allan Library*

Right: Winson Green in August 2001, as an EMU speeds past the site of the former station that has been comprehensively demolished. Only the parting of the tracks around the former station platforms indicates the fact that a substantial station once existed here. *Author*

Right: The very limited timetable via Sutton Park in September 1964.

BIRMINGHAM, SUTTON PARK AND WALSALL
WEEKDAYS ONLY

Miles		a.m.	a.m.		SO p.m.	SO p.m.		p.m.	p.m.	
0	BIRMINGHAM New St. dep.	7 15	8 5	.	12 20	1 10	.	5 40	6 49	.
2	Saltley	7 19	8 9	...	12 24	1 14	...	5 44	6 53	...
5¼	Castle Bromwich	7 24	8 14	..	12 29	1 19	..	5 49	6 58	...
8½	Penns	7 31	8 21	...	12 36	1 26	..	5 56	7 5	...
11	Sutton Park	7 37	8 27	.	12 42	1 32	.	6 2	7 11	.
13½	Streetly	7 43	8 32	...	12 47	1 37	...	6 7	7 16	...
15¾	Aldridge	7 48	8 37	.	12 52	1 42	.	6 12	7 21	...
19	WALSALL arr.	7 56	8 45	...	12 59	1 49	...	6 19	7 28	...

Miles		a.m.	a.m.	SO a.m.	SX a.m.	SO p.m.		p.m.	p.m.	
0	WALSALL dep.	.	6 45	8 0	8 0	1 46	.	5 53	6 54	.
3½	Aldridge	...	6 53	8 8	8 8	1 53	.	6 0	7 1	...
5¾	Streetly	.	6 58	8 13	8 13	1 57	.	6 5	7 5	...
8	Sutton Park	...	7 2	8 17	8 17	2 2	.	6 11	7 10	...
10¼	Penns	.	7 7	8 22	8 22	2 6	.	6 15	7 14	.
13¾	Castle Bromwich	...	7 13	8 28	8 28	2 13	...	6 24	7 21	...
17	Saltley	.	7 21	8 37	8 35	2 21	...	6 32	7 29	...
19	BIRMINGHAM New St. arr.	...	7 28	8 42	8 40	2 27	...	6 39	7 35	...

SO—Saturdays only.

SX—Saturdays excepted.

Right: 'Black 5' 4-6-0 No 45333, with an empty return excursion for the Boy Scouts Jubilee Jamboree in Sutton Park, restarts from a signal stop at Streetly station on Sunday, 4 August 1957. The station closed in 1965 and the buildings have subsequently been demolished. *M. Mensing*

Above: Ex-LNWR 0-8-0 No 49361 struggles past Sutton Park station with the 9.30am Water Orton-Wolverhampton freight on 7 March 1964. Only a few of this once-numerous class of locomotive survived at this time. The station opened in 1879 and closed to passenger traffic, along with all others on this line, in January 1965. *P. Riley*

Below: The station buildings were still extant at Sutton Park, but in a very dilapidated condition, when this view was taken in the summer of 2001, almost four decades after the buildings were last in use for passenger trains. Post Office sidings at the station remained in operation until 1995. *Author's collection*

the 1960s. Some of the stations to be closed boasted considerable staff and in a few cases even had refreshment facilities. Yet more often than not, in later years, they were increasingly out of touch with the modern world, with their shabby paintwork, grimy buildings, gas-lit platforms and infrequent steam-operated services.

Some examples of closures prior to World War 1 include Rushall, Ryder's Hay and Wednesfield Heath; originally all these stations were located in rural areas. Birchills, Bradley & Moxley, Monmore Green and Ocker Hill were amongst a handful of stations that saw passenger traffic end, as an economy measure, during the war. Church Road and Sutton Town were amongst facilities closed in the 1920s, while Somerset Road was one of the very few closures in the 1930s.

Brighton Road, Soho Road, Handsworth Wood and Newton Road were amongst the casualties of World War 2. However, closure of all six intermediate stations on the line from Saltley to King's Norton in 1941, including Camp Hill, Moseley and Lifford, was a particular blow that has yet to be rectified.

Winson Green was one of a number of stations, including Monument Lane, Spon Lane, Ettingshall Road and Albion, which closed on the busy Stour Valley line in the 1950s and 1960s.

The list grows as the Beeching cuts, particularly between 1965 and 1968, depleted the number of stations in the area. A particular loss was the closure of all the stations on the line from Birmingham to Water Orton and on the former Midland route from Birmingham to Walsall, with the loss of well-known stations such as Saltley, Castle Bromwich, Penns, Sutton Park, Streetly and Aldridge. Willenhall and Darlaston were other notable towns lost to the railway map at this time.

The closure of Birmingham Racecourse led to the end of special trains to Bromford Bridge in 1965. The Hawthorns Halt, opened in 1931 to serve specials to West Bromwich Albion football ground, closed in April 1968. After this date the list of individual stations closed on lines that remained operational largely ceased, later closures being the result of rationalisation, or improvements, rather than cuts. The trend is now for new and reopened stations in the area, which will hopefully continue if capacity allows. As closed stations are dispersed throughout Birmingham and the Black Country, it may be possible to see others reopen in the future, all helping to relieve traffic congestion.

Right: Ex-LNWR 0-8-0 No 49210 with a northbound freight trundles through Penns station on 5 September 1959. Passenger services were run down, until only a few trains in each direction served stations on this route by 1964. This station closed, along with the others on this line, in 1965. *M. Mensing*

Left: A two-car Gloucester RCW DMU on the 1.46pm Walsall-Birmingham New Street train leaves Penns station and passes the goods depot, which was separated from the passenger station, on 2 October 1959. All the station buildings have subsequently been demolished, including the new attachments to the goods shed seen in this view. *M. Mensing*

Below: Class 4F 0-6-0 No 44562 passes through Castle Bromwich station with an eastbound freight on 4 May 1963. The station buildings dated from 1901 and survived until closure in 1968. *G. Robinson*

Upper right: Another view of Castle Bromwich, in 1951, when the neat and tidy station provided a refreshment room. A large platform sign, in four languages, advises persons to 'Alight here for the fair', which was in this case the nearby British Industries Fair, held at an exhibition centre to the north of the station. *Ian Allan Library*

Centre right: All that remains of Castle Bromwich station today are some platform abutments adjoining the main lines, as this view taken in August 2001 shows. *Author*

Lower right: Ex-MR '2P' 4-4-0 No 40511 and Ivatt Class 4 2-6-0 No 43017 coupled tender-to-tender, a rather unusual combination of motive power, with a collection of empty stock, pass Saltley station on 26 April 1958 on the down line. Saltley station was opened by the MR in 1854, replaced by a new station in 1899 and closed in March 1968. *M. Mensing*

Below: 1930s services and fares.

LIFFORD (Worcester). 119 miles. Fares, 23/7a, 14/2c; Return, 47/2a, 28/4c. From London as to Birmingham (New Street), thence about 25 minutes, 5 times daily.

SUTTON PARK (Staffs). 129¼ miles. No through fares. From London as to Birmingham (New Street), thence 30 minutes, about 6 times daily.

CASTLE BROMWICH (Warwick). 126¼ miles. Fares, 23/2a, 13/11c; Return, 46/4a, 27/10c. From St. Pancras, as to Stockingford, thence 30 minutes, about 4 times daily. Pop. 1,074.

SALTLEY (Warwick). 118 miles. Fares, 23/2a, 13/11c; Return, 46/4a, 27/10c. From London as to Birmingham (New Street), thence by Midland Railway, 8 minutes, frequent service. Pop. 31,416.

Above: A gas-lit Saltley station in February 1968, shortly before closure the following month. The nearby gas works was demolished soon afterwards changing for ever the industrial landscape in this area. A canal passed under the station. *A. Muckley*

Left: Smethwick West, known as Smethwick Junction in GWR days, was one of the last station closures in the area, with services ending in September 1996 when a new interchange station opened nearby. The platforms still survived when this view was taken in August 2000. After Smethwick Galton Bridge opened, one train in each direction still called at Smethwick West on Saturdays for a year, as the proper statutory closure procedures had not been observed. *Author*

23 **Lost Link and Loop Lines**

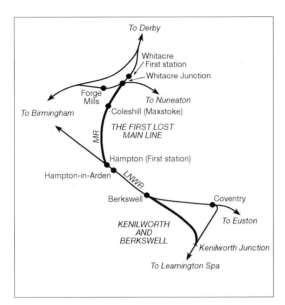

A number of link and loop lines existed in the area. Some were built mainly to cope with the diversity and volume of freight movements. They were particularly useful during World War 2 in providing diversionary routes when air raid damage closed sections of line.

The First Lost Main Line

The Hampton-Whitacre line ran via Coleshill and opened in August 1839. The Birmingham & Derby Junction Railway built this 6½-mile section of route as part of a main line from London to Derby. Heavy tolls for use of the L&B part of the journey led to construction of a new, more direct line to Derby and as far back as 1842, the Hampton-Whitacre Junction line lost its trunk route status and was singled. The passenger service became limited to one train daily in each direction and the line finally closed to passengers at the end of 1916, as a wartime economy measure. As such, it was the first major section of main line in the Midlands to lose its passenger services.

Coleshill, the only intermediate station on the line, remained open for goods and was renamed Maxstoke by the LMS in 1923. Through freight services ceased in 1930, while a bridge failure in 1934 prevented through use in any event. The local goods service to Maxstoke ended in April 1939 and the station was subsequently demolished. Yet parts of the line remained: a northern section became a crippled wagon store, while two miles of the southern part reopened during World War 2 to sand pits, which were required for the construction of airfields in the area. This section of line was lifted in 1952, except for a short siding which lasted until 1970. All use of the remaining northern end of the line ceased in the 1960s and the track was removed. Today, much of the often heavily constructed former main line is overgrown by mature trees, creating a distinctive feature in the landscape, while the attractive original passenger station building at Hampton-in-Arden is still in existence.

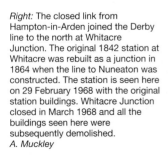

Right: The closed link from Hampton-in-Arden joined the Derby line to the north at Whitacre Junction. The original 1842 station at Whitacre was rebuilt as a junction in 1864 when the line to Nuneaton was constructed. The station is seen here on 29 February 1968 with the original station buildings. Whitacre Junction closed in March 1968 and all the buildings seen here were subsequently demolished.
A. Muckley

Left: The attractive stone band within this substantial bridge gives a clue to the fact that it once spanned a main line. This bridge, to the north of Hampton-in-Arden, was one of many equally imposing structures built by the Birmingham & Derby Junction Railway in the early 1840s. This view of the bridge, together with the very heavily overgrown cutting, was taken in August 2000. *Author's collection*

Below: What's in a name? A Birmingham-Leicester stopping train calls at Coleshill station on 29 February 1968. Originally this station was called Forge Mills, but after closure of the original Coleshill station to passengers on the old main line it was renamed Coleshill in 1923 by the newly formed LMS. The original Coleshill was renamed Maxstoke and remained open for freight until 1930. The station in this view closed to passengers in 1965, to all traffic in 1968 and was subsequently demolished. *A. Muckley*

Kenilworth & Berkswell

The double-track LNWR link from Kenilworth Junction to Berkswell Junction was opened in March 1884 and led to the doubling of the line to the south of Kenilworth. The route enabled trains, particularly freight trains, running to the south from Birmingham to avoid the busy station of Coventry. The line had no intermediate stations and was identified in the Beeching Report for closure, together with the direct line from Kenilworth to Coventry. A rationalisation of

Above: 'Black 5' 4-6-0 No 44833 climbs the 1 in 100 grade on the Kenilworth Junction-Berkswell line with the 7.57am Leamington Spa-Manchester service in August 1964. *P. Riley*

Right: Kenilworth Junction, where the line to Berkswell once ran under the ivy-covered brick arches. Class 47 No 47622 passes with the 08.00 Newcastle-Poole train on 26 April 1986. At this time, plans to reopen the link were being considered in conjunction with a Warwickshire super coal pit that was being proposed in the area. These plans came to nothing and today most of the former route is used as a footpath. *C. Underhill*

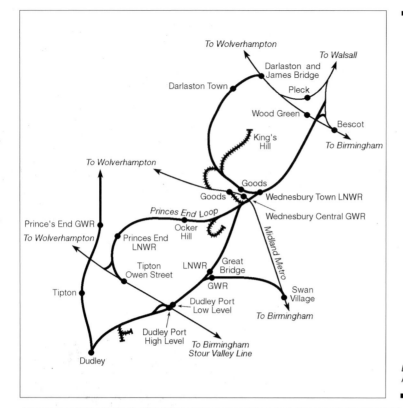

	DUDLEY PORT, PRINCES END, and WEDNESBURY.— London and North Western.											
Miles	**Up.** High Level,	**Week Days.**					Miles	**Down.**	**Week Days.**			
		mrn	mrn	aft	aft	aft			mrn	mrn	aft	aft
	Dudley Port ......dep.	8 50	1022	1220	3 20	6 52		Wednesbury ......dep.	7 38	1052	1255	3 42
¼	Tipton	8 52	1025	1223	3 23	6 54	¼	Ocker Hill	7 41	1055	1258	3 45
2	Princes End............	8 55	1028	1226	3 26	6 57	1½	Princes End	7 44	1058	1 1	3 48
3	Ocker Hill	8 58	1031	1229	3 29	7 0	3	Tipton 450	7 47	11 2	1 4	3 51
3¼	Wednesbury 447 ..arr.	9 0	1035	1232	3 32	7 2	3¼	Dudley Port (H.L.) 447	7 49	11 4	1 6	3 53

cross-country services, so that more trains could include Coventry as one of their stops, led to a reprieve of the line to Coventry, but the cut-off line to Berkswell closed to passengers in January 1965 and to all traffic four years later. A small southern section has become overgrown and in 2002 a short section remained as a siding at Berkswell, which on occasions has been used to stable the Royal Train, but most of the route is now used as a footpath.

Princes End

The Princes End branch was opened in September 1863 by the LNWR from its newly built station at Wednesbury. The double-track branch curved round 2¾ miles, via Ocker Hill and Princes End, to provide links to both the south and north on the Stour Valley line at Tipton. Although used for a time by Walsall-Wolverhampton trains, passenger services over the line were first withdrawn in November 1890. After local opposition they were restored in 1895. However, they were withdrawn again as a wartime economy measure by the LNWR in January 1916. The

demolition of Princes End station helped to ensure that passenger services were not restored again.

Freight use was considerable and through freight endured much longer, until April 1981, while a section of line from Wednesbury to the power station at Ocker Hill, survived until December 1989.

The branch and other associated loops and links (including a link between Wednesbury and Darlaston that also lost its passenger services early in 1887 but survived for freight for much longer) enabled great flexibility for train operations in the area. To some extent, if you were looking to identify the heart of lost railways in this country it might well be said to be in this general area. Indeed, there are plans for Wednesbury to become an interchange for lines on the Midland Metro that would again link to many destinations once served by train.

The other station at Princes End was to be found on the ex-GWR line from Dudley to Priestfield. This station, which was named as Prince's End & Coseley, closed to passengers in July 1962 and also met its end by demolition.

Right: The substantial Wednesbury Town station, looking north on 13 August 1947, with LMS No 6661 on a motor train, the 6.42pm Walsall-Dudley service. In its heyday, trains from Wednesbury Town ran to Darlaston, Walsall, Tipton and Dudley. The platform to the left of this view remains, but all other parts of the station have long since been demolished. In some respects this important former junction, all currently closed, could perhaps be said to be at the very heart of lost lines in this country. *W. A. Camwell*

Right: On Saturday, 13 August 1955 the 1.35pm Stourbridge-Wolverhampton local was worked by Class 5101 2-6-2T No 5165 and is seen here near Prince's End & Coseley station. This alternative GWR station, serving Prince's End, survived that on the LNWR Princes End (spelt without an apostrophe) loop line by over 45 years before it also closed in 1962. *M. Hale*

Right: The site of the ex-LNWR station at Wednesbury Town, looking south towards the Princes End line in the summer of 2000. There are plans for freight use through the station as part of the Walsall-Stourbridge Junction line reopening. Plans for Wednesbury to become an interchange on the Midland Metro, with trams using sections of the line south to Dudley, are also proposed and consideration has even been given to using parts of the old loop line to Darlaston. *Author's collection*

Far right: The Walsall-Stourbridge line at Wednesbury Town crosses a road close to the former Town station. At one time, this route was heavily used, particularly by freight trains, but closed in March 1993. It is clear that it was not in use when this view was taken in August 2000, but there are plans for reopening, to enable freight trains to avoid the central Birmingham area. *Author*

STOP when lights show

This was an extensively used network and the heavy traffic, in particular freight operations, led to the construction of a considerable number of locomotive sheds in the area. One of the most difficult workings for steam locomotives was the nearby Lickey Incline, where reserves of banking engines were once required.

After the railways were nationalised, rationalisation and dieselisation began to take place. Steam gradually gave way to diesel, both multiple-units and locomotives, and later to electric traction. By the 1960s, most passenger services were becoming diesel operated; by 1966 regular steam working ended in Birmingham and the Black Country and the last steam trains officially ran in the area during the following year. These changes had a profound effect on the engine sheds that were spread throughout the network.

Of the sheds that survived into the LMR, Walsall, which was located at Ryecroft Junction, was allocated almost 60 engines in 1950, but was the first to close to steam in 1958, although it remained as a DMU depot until 1967. Bournville had a roundhouse built by the Midland Railway and over 30 engines were allocated here in 1950; it was the next to go, in February 1960, and like Walsall, was subsequently demolished. It was a foretaste of what was to come. Monument Lane was a six-road straight shed that was allocated more than 30 engines in 1950, but closed in January 1962 and

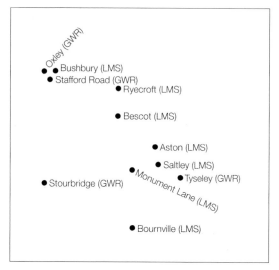

was later demolished. Aston with over 50 engines in 1950 and Bushbury with over 40 at the same period, both closed in 1965 and both were demolished. Bescot, which in 1959 had an allocation in excess of 80 engines, closed in 1966, although part of the former steam shed still stands.

Saltley shed was built on the roundhouse principle. The shed had about 180 mainly freight locomotives in

Left: Walsall shed was located on one of the triangular areas of land formed within the lines of Ryecroft Junction. Here, ex-LNWR 0-8-0 No 9326 is seen outside the decrepit-looking shed in 1947. The shed was the first major steam closure in the area, in 1958, and today the site is covered with mature trees. *F. Moss*

Upper right: Bournville shed, opened by the MR in 1895, was the next major closure in 1960. The former Midland shed is seen here on 2 March 1935 with an ex-Midland 2-4-0, by then numbered 20002 by the LMS. *H. C. Casserley*

Centre right: The LNWR opened Monument Lane shed in 1858. The view here shows one of the ex-LNWR 0-6-2T 'Coal Tanks' in BR livery as No 58900. The shed, which was coded by BR as 3E, was downgraded after World War 2 and was finally closed as 21E in 1962. It has since been demolished and the area redeveloped. *C. B. Golding*

Below: Aston shed was renewed by the LNWR in 1882 and could be home to more than 60 locomotives. The shed is seen here on Sunday, 30 June 1963, with an array of locomotives in steam. Nos 45545, 42964, 44838, 45838, 45186, 75034 and 45048 are all seen in this view. Originally coded 3D by BR, this was changed to 21D in 1960 and to 2J in 1963. It closed in 1965 and was subsequently demolished. *A. W. Martin*

Upper left: Ex-LNWR 2-4-2T No 46712 is seen here in the open at Bushbury shed, Wolverhampton, in September 1951. The shed was coded as 3B, which was changed to 21C and finally to 2K in 1963. The building was reroofed by BR before closure in 1965. *D. Taylor*

Right: Saltley shed opened in 1855 and at one time, over 200 locomotives were allocated here. This shed was of the enclosed roundhouse type and accommodated mainly freight locomotives. The BR shedcode was changed from 21A to 2E in 1963. Here, LMS Compound 4-4-0 No 41180 and Stanier Class 8F No 48687 are seen at rest, as Stanier '8F' 2-8-0 No 48700 is being turned, on 3 August 1955. *R. O. Hodge*

Centre left: Ex-LNWR 0-8-0 No 49371 is seen in the centre of this view at Bescot shed in May 1950. The powerful engine was one of many that were used to convey huge amounts of freight in the area. The Bescot shedcode was changed from 3A to 21B in 1960 and from 21B to 2F in 1963. Part of the steam shed still stands unused, while Bescot remains in use as an EWS diesel depot. *P. B. Whitehouse*

Left: Another ex-LNWR 0-8-0 standard heavy freight locomotive, No 49173, is seen dead at Bescot shed on 19 September 1964. The cabside yellow stripe indicated that the engine was not to work under the overhead electric catenary south of Crewe. Note the floodlights on the shed roof, designed to assist 24-hour working. Bescot steam shed closed in 1966. *Ian Allan Library*

Right: Saltley shed roundhouse with two ex-Crosti '9F' 2-10-0s, No 92024 and another unidentified, and Class 8F 2-8-0 No 48339, seen in August 1966. The shed housed mainly freight locomotives. The Franco-Crosti boilers and pre-heaters were not a success and the locomotives so fitted were converted to normal arrangements, although they retained their distinctive looks. *I. J. Hodson*

1950, although this had reduced to under 50 by 1965. Saltley was the main LMR shed in the Birmingham area. It survived until the official end of steam, in March 1967, when the full electric service began, and was subsequently demolished.

The former GWR sheds to be found in the area, included the famous Wolverhampton Stafford Road depot. Dating from the 1860s, when it was converted to standard gauge, the original shed was replaced in 1907 by a new shed. In 1947, about 75 locomotives were allocated here, but it was the first major GWR shed closed in the area in September 1963 and the dilapidated buildings were soon demolished. The adjacent railway workshops closed the following year. Stourbridge Junction had 28 pits in its roundhouse and was built in 1926 to replace an earlier smaller shed. In 1950, about 85 engines were on shed here. The shed closed in July 1966 and was subsequently demolished. Tyseley shed dated from 1908 and in 1950 had an allocation of almost 120 engines, of which 40 were pannier tanks. The 84E shed code was changed to 2A when the LMR took over. The shed officially closed to steam in 1966 and the final roundhouse was demolished in 1969. Oxley shed at Wolverhampton

was opened in 1907 and was of the roundhouse type. It had over 100 locomotives in 1947. It was taken over by the LMR in 1963 and, with several other sheds in the area, was recoded, in this case from 84B to 2B. It was one of the last former GWR steam sheds to close, in March 1967, on the official demise of steam in the area.

The remains of the former GWR Tyseley steam shed have been equipped with specialist railway engineering machinery to enable preserved steam locomotives to continue to be repaired. The site is the home of the Tyseley Locomotive Works and Birmingham Railway Museum, and a considerable number of preserved locomotives can be found there.

Left: A brace of '8F' 2-8-0s, Nos 48220 and 48192, are flanked by '9F' 2-10-0 No 92136 and 'Black 5' No 44920 inside Saltley roundhouse in August 1966. The shed was damaged in World War 2 and much of the roof was subsequently removed and the whole building was latterly in a poor state of repair. It was closed in 1967 and subsequently demolished. *I. J. Hodson*

Left: The GWR's most powerful passenger locomotives were the four-cylinder 4-6-0 'King' class. Here, No 6009 *King Charles II* is seen towards the end of its life, on 19 February 1961, moving away from the coaling stage at Wolverhampton, after being re-coaled. The coaling stage was situated near to Stafford Road shed, coded 84A, and was demolished, along with the shed, after closure in 1963. *H. O. Fletcher*

Above: Stourbridge shed, 84F, was recoded to 2C after it was transferred to the LMR. A line-up of ex-GWR 0-6-0PTs is seen here on Sunday, 1 May 1966. The shed closed in the summer of that year and was subsequently demolished. *N. E. Preedy*

Left: There had been an engine shed at Stourbridge since 1870. By November 1959, when this view of ex-GWR diesel railcars Nos W15W and W8W was taken, it had been modernised to include a diesel refuelling facility, but this was not to save the shed which closed in 1966. These railcars had operated the 'Town Bus' on the Stourbridge branch, but by this time they were stored out of use. *T. J. Farebrother*

Left: The main shed at Tyseley was of the enclosed roundhouse type. Part is seen here in 1956 with ROD 2-8-0 No 3012, constructed to a Robinson Great Central Railway design for the War Department during World War 1. No 3012 is seen here simmering between 2-6-2T No 4155 and 2-8-0 No 2856. All of these distinctive GCR-designed GWR locomotives were scrapped by 1958. *Ian Allan Library*

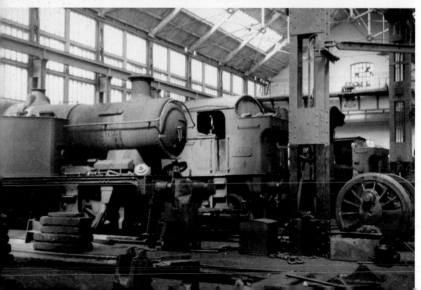

Left: Inside the repair shop, known as 'The Factory', which was attached to Tyseley shed, on 13 August 1950. In the 1950s, when this view was taken, over 40 pannier tanks were allocated to Tyseley. It officially closed as a major BR steam shed in 1966 but today repairs to steam locomotives are still undertaken here, now home of Tyseley Locomotive Works. *M. J. Thomas*

Above: Tyseley, with outside-framed 'Dukedog' 4-4-0 No 9015 stored dead in the yard, with the 98,000-gallon water tank in the background. Although this photograph is not dated, all surviving engines of this class were withdrawn by 1960. *P. B. Whitehouse*

Below: Wolverhampton Oxley shed was opened in 1907 because of overcrowding at the Stafford Road shed. This view, with 0-6-0PTs and 'Castle' class 4-6-0 No 5089 *Westminster Abbey*, was taken in the summer of 1964. Oxley shed was coded by BR as 84B, but was recoded in 1963 as 2B. The ex-GWR shed was of the roundhouse type and was one of the last to close in the area, in 1967. *J. Hunt*

25 Birmingham and its Beautiful Borderlands

There were many attractions close at hand to Birmingham and the Black Country. In addition to football grounds, greyhound stadiums and racecourses, Sutton Park and Dudley Zoo, which until 1992 had a miniature zoo railway, became local destinations for many to visit by train. The railways were quick to realise the potential of the area and the SSR tried to lease Dudley Castle. The limestone caves at Dudley were also illuminated as an early attraction, soon after the railway opened to the town.

The railways also provided the means of escaping to the nearby rolling countryside. The Great Western Railway, ever creative, aimed to tempt passengers to visit the surrounding countryside and advertised the area as 'Birmingham and its Beautiful Borderlands'.

The attractive posters and maps enlivened many a drab Black Country station. The genteel tourist industry of Royal Leamington Spa and the rolling countryside of the Severn Valley were promoted as potential visitor destinations by the GWR, together with golf links and even fox hunting meets.

Right: Ivatt Class 2 2-6-0 No 46470 banks a Halesowen-Stourbridge goods train out of Halesowen on 3 October 1966. The line, which closed in 1969, passed through surprisingly attractive countryside, sometimes known as the 'lungs of Birmingham'. At Rubery, tourist facilities developed, with trams running to the scenic Lickey Hills. *R. Siviter*

Left: The 6.13pm Stourbridge-Wolverhampton train catches the evening sun with Dudley Castle Hill in the background on 8 August 1955. The castle and the zoo at Dudley were popular attractions, close to Dudley station. Recently ex-works, the Collett 2-6-2T, No 5191, in this view had been painted black, but lacked its BR emblem. The line seen here closed to passengers in 1962. *M. Hale*

Right: BR Class 3MT 2-6-2T No 82030 heads the 8.38am Bewdley-Worcester train leaving Stourport-on-Severn on 24 April 1958. A number of excursions were run to Stourport-on-Severn from Birmingham and the Black Country in connection with the town's September carnival. All passenger services to the town ended by 1970. *A. A. Vickers*

STRATFORD-UPON-AVON

Welcombe Hotel

An elegant Country House hotel surrounded by English parkland in the heart of Shakespeare's Warwickshire.

OPEN THROUGHOUT

THE YEAR

TELEPHONE
Stratford upon-Avon 3611

The Resident Manager will be happy to send full particulars.

BRITISH TRANSPORT HOTELS

Above: The LMS Welcombe Hotel near Stratford-upon-Avon on 4 July 1931, in its opening year. The building on the far right of this view was subsequently demolished. The LMS highlighted the countryside around the hotel with maps extending to Kenilworth. Although no longer in railway ownership, it still operates as a hotel. *Ian Allan Library*

Right: Emerging from Foley Park Tunnel, preserved '5700' class 0-6-0PT No 5764 heads along the Severn Valley Railway on 9 September 1979. The SVR runs through delightful countryside, as this view shows. *Brian Morrison*

Not to be outdone, the LMS opened the Welcombe Hotel near Stratford-upon-Avon in 1931 and extended it in 1933. The hotel was served in 1932 by a unique bus that could run on both road and rail. The 'Ro-Railer', as it was called, was built by the LMS, running on track to Stratford-upon-Avon and then on the road to the hotel. The hotel is no longer in railway ownership, but remains open.

Kinver Edge was a popular destination for many a Black Country worker and was served by the Kinver Light Railway from 1901 until its closure in 1930. This was in many respects an electric tramway that ran along the road for much of its route. Trams also served the Lickey Hills and connections could be made at Rubery. The wilder parts of Cannock Chase were also destinations for day trips into the countryside.

Special trains ran to locations relatively close by, for example to Stourport-on-Severn for the carnival, and to Dudley Zoo. Other excursions ran further afield, to a wide range of holiday destinations, in some cases over miles of line now closed such as the Somerset & Dorset Joint Railway to Bournemouth West.

Much of the countryside around Birmingham is protected by Green Belt legislation, remains beautiful and some can still be discovered by train.

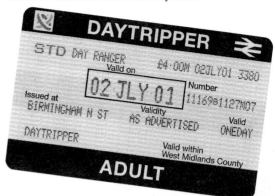

26 Revolution and Renaissance

The early roots of the Industrial Revolution may be traced to the Ironbridge area, but soon included Birmingham and the Black Country. Today, the original heavy industrial emphasis of the area has declined considerably. A view over Birmingham now displays a vibrant commercial and cultural centre and many of the old industrial landmarks in the area are no more.

The railways also suffered years of decline, but from their lowest ebb in the early 1960s they began to adapt to the new image. In 1967, electrification through New Street heralded a new beginning. In 1978, Cross City electric services saw Five Ways station reopened and by 1984 Dudley was at least reinstated on the railway map with a nearby station. Snow Hill reopened in 1987 and passenger services recommenced on two routes to Walsall in 1989 and 1998. Gradually the railways were

seen as a fundamental asset to the area. As road congestion inexorably grew, they are once again a significant component in the economic prosperity and regeneration of the area. Between 1997 and 1998 there was an overall 8.5% increase in passengers arriving at the main rail stations in Birmingham city centre. It is clear that ever more passengers are using the railways in the area, including those services that were once threatened with closure.

The restoration of two alternative routes from Birmingham to London, from Snow Hill or from New Street, are other indications of the railway's revival. There are plans to reinstate four tracks of the ex-GWR main line between Tyseley and Dorridge, together with capacity improvements on other routes. There are new freight initiatives, including the reopening of the line

Right: Two of the original cast seats from the old Snow Hill station are currently in use at the new Snow Hill station. The distinctive GWR and BR (W) seat designs are seen here, still being put to good use in 2002 when this view was taken, 150 years after the first station opened on this site. *Author's collection*

Right: Midland Metro No 12 glides along the track once used by Paddington-Birkenhead trains, in September 2001 at Jewellery Quarter, near the site of the old Hockley station. The lines seen here were once all closed and lifted, but it is now a busy railway artery again. The lines closest to the camera are being used by Snow Hill-Stourbridge Junction trains. *Author*

Left: A close-up of the Tipton end entrance to the Dudley Canal Tunnel on 6 May 1967. High above the canal tunnel the bridge once carried the main Dudley-Wolverhampton railway line. The railways were originally serious rivals to the canals, yet the railway here closed to all traffic in 1968, while the canal, which was designed primarily for freight, continues with its trade in sightseers. The location seen here is now part of the Black Country Living Museum. *A. Muckley*

between Stourbridge and Walsall and perhaps on to Lichfield. Historically, changes have not been rapid, but the future is set fair for a continued railway renaissance in the area.

In other forms of transport, a much extended Midland Metro into Birmingham city centre, with up to 10 routes, including links that may use part of disused railways between Walsall and Wolverhampton, Wednesbury and Round Oak and the Darlaston loop, is under consideration. The tram is back. The restoration and maintenance of much of the remaining canal network, for tourism, all go to show that even if the Industrial Revolution is at an end, a transport revolution is continuing in the region.

Yet as the area looks to the future, it is also able to look to its past. A wealth of museums have opened and many railway and industrial legacies that were considered commonplace a relatively short time ago are now part of this area's rich and fascinating heritage. The railway centre at Tyseley, the 'Think Tank' museum in Birmingham, containing 'Princes Coronation' Pacific *City of Birmingham*, the Black Country Museum at Dudley and preserved railways at Chasewater and further away in the Severn Valley, are just some of the attractions that provide a glimpse of the remarkable and fascinating transport history of Birmingham and the Black Country.

Above: Brownhills West station, on the Colliery Line as the Chasewater Railway is known, to reflect its location in the Cannock coal field, with a preserved DMU showing a Longbridge destination blind in June 2001. Longbridge is now on the Cross City electrified line and DMUs, such as in this view, that were commonplace just a few years ago are now part of the heritage of the area. *Author's collection*

Below: Here, No 7029 *Clun Castle*, right, and No 4079 *Pendennis Castle*, left, are seen at Tyseley shed in March 1967. Several steam locomotives escaped the scrapyard on the demise of steam, to provide great pleasure for future generations. The Birmingham Railway Museum and Tyseley Locomotive Works, on the site of the former Tyseley steam shed, continue to store and repair a range of preserved locomotives. The centre also runs a number of main line steam railtours and a full education service. *P. B. Whitehouse*